EMERGENCY MANAGEMENT
of the
NATIONAL ECONOMY

VOLUME I

THE NATURE
OF
ECONOMIC MOBILIZATION

Louis C. Hunter, Ph. D.

WILDSIDE PRESS

FOREWORD

A FRAMEWORK FOR MOBILIZATION PREPAREDNESS IN AN AGE OF PERIL

It is a privilege and an opportunity to participate in the program of the Industrial College of the Armed Forces. The studies you are about to undertake are an integral part of our national security. It is my purpose in these brief observations to:

1. Set out the basic premises of our defense mobilization planning.

2. Outline its program objectives.

3. Indicate the urgency of your studies.

PREMISES

These are the premises on which our defense mobilization planning is predicated:

1. We are in the midst—not of a year or a decade—but of an age of peril.

Never before in our history have we as a Nation been confronted with as serious a threat to our basic freedoms. Yet we must not lose sight of American fundamentals. In the words of President Eisenhower:

The truth is that our danger cannot be fixed or confined to a specific instant.

We live in an age of peril.

We must think and plan and provide so as to live through this age in freedom—in ways that do not undermine our freedom even as we strive to defend it.

2. We must proceed from a position of strength as, during this age of peril, we deal with Communist Russia and with her satellites.

We all hope that, step by step, through the United Nations, and in other ways, it will be possible to lessen the possibility of war and to move in the direction of a peaceful world.

We know, however, that our Nation must be strong both physically and spiritually if we are to persuade Communist Russia that war will not pay—and in the event rationality does not prevail—to win any war waged against us.

3. We must be prepared to deal with a broad diversity of war conditions.

We cannot anticipate the precise form of war that may be thrust upon us. We must be prepared, however, to deal with such reasonable possibilities as "cold war", "local" hot war, and all-out atomic war. Flexibility and adaptability must characterize our defense thinking.

4. We must be prepared to shift from a civilian economy to a war economy in a very short period of time.

Never again will we have the time that we had after the start of World War II to mobilize both our material and our human resources.

Either we get ready to mobilize these resources now, or we will wake up to the fact that there are certain things we could have done in dealing with an enemy which it will be impossible to do because of the terribly swift pace that will characterize any war of the future.

We can be guilty of the sin of "too little and too late" in a period of defense mobilization just as surely as we could be guilty of such a sin during a war period.

5. We must be prepared for a devastating attack on the continental United States.

We know that Soviet Russia has the capability of attack on continental United States.

We know that preparedness for such an attack can save an untold number of human lives, and in addition can assure our ability to continue a substantial portion of our war production and production essential for the holding together of our civilian economy.

We must, therefore, place major emphasis on such a preparedness program.

OBJECTIVES

Accordingly, our defense mobilization program is designed to:

1. Maintain a broad and strong mobilization base.

No consideration will be permitted to stand in the way of reaching this objective for our military strength ultimately rests upon our ability to produce the complex weapons of modern warfare.

But we must define very carefully just what we mean by the maintenance of the mobilization base if we are to avoid costly and useless programs.

The maintenance of the base does not mean—and has never meant—keeping in full operation all production lines which were required to meet the peak needs of full mobilization during the Korean conflict. It does not mean maintaining facilities to produce weapons which would be obsolete in the event of a new war. Nor does it necessarily mean keeping less efficient producers in operation.

The maintenance of the base does mean, however, that we should do everything possible to have in readiness that combination of facilities, production equipment, and skilled workers whose production, together with any existing military reserve of weapons, can meet rapidly accelerating wartime requirements.

2. Identify, in as systematic and realistic a manner as possible, the gaps in our mobilization base.

Our Nation has never succeeded in doing a satisfactory job of identifying in advance just what our requirements would be in the event of mobilization. As a result, we have never been in a position where we could do an intelligent and effective job of preparedness. If we are not sure that we are going to need a particular item, or if we have only a vague notion of the quantity that would be needed, we are not going to be able to do very much about getting ourselves in a position where we will be ready, within a very short period of time after the emergency strikes, to manufacture the item in the required quantities.

3. Complete our expansion goals just as rapidly as possible.

Since 1950 the Executive Branch has had available a revolving fund of $2,100,000,000 which the Congress stated could be used to help finance projects for filling in gaps in the mobilization base. It has also had authority to grant rapid tax amortization for projects directly related to our defense mobilization needs.

In order to provide a standard against which to judge requests for assistance from the $2,100,000,000 revolving fund and requests for rapid tax write-off the Government established more than 200 expansion goals for particular materials and products. In reality this was an effort to identify the extent of the gaps in our mobilization base in these areas. Present reports indicate that we have reached our goals in most of these areas. Since the mobilization program must be adjusted to changing circumstances, the expansion goals must be subjected to frequent review and revision.

4. Reach the goal for the stockpiling of critical materials in the shortest possible period of time without interfering with the current defense program and without creating undue hardship within the civilian economy.

The purpose of our stockpile program is clear, namely, to put us in a position where we will not be plagued by materials bottlenecks if it becomes necessary for us to move quickly from civilian to war production.

The Government has an investment of more than $16 billion in the stockpile. More than three fourths of our total minimum stockpile objectives are now on hand. Additional large quantities are on order.

Here again, it is necessary for us to review our goals from time to time. Some may be raised and others lowered. If there is a reasonable doubt, however, as to whether an objective should be set at a higher figure or a lower figure, the doubt will be resolved in favor of the higher figure.

5. Provide the leadership for programs that will result in our doing something about manpower shortages before it is too late for us to act.

We are providing for the expansion of defense plant capacity now because we know that it must be done before and not after all-out mobilization.

What is true of defense plants is even more true of manpower. We know, for example, that today the combined demands of our mobilization program and the civilian economy are such that we do not have a sufficient number of scientists and engineers. If we should be plunged into all-out mobilization the situation would be critical.

We cannot in advance provide for all of the specialized manpower needs that would confront us in the event of all-out mobilization. Human effort cannot be stockpiled; but skills can be developed. And if we can eliminate or moderate the skilled manpower shortages of the present stage of partial mobilization, we will have moved in the direction of an adequate manpower mobilization base.

6. Stimulate business and community organizations and individual citizens to do those things now that, if done, would result in saving lives and lessening the destruction of property, if we should be attacked.

Let us keep in mind that Soviet Russia has the capability to attack us.

We know that an adequate preparedness program will save an untold number of lives, will make it possible for the essential functions of Government to be continued, and will likewise enable us to continue our vital production. The major facets of such a program include: an adequate early warning system of the imminence of enemy attack; steps to improve the ability of industry to continue vital production in the event of attack; measures to provide for necessary health, safety and community facilities.

URGENCY

While you may be dealing with hypothetical situations and historical matters in pursuing your studies, the end result of your training is urgently required. You are not engaged in mere self-improvement. The danger confronting us was stated succinctly by the President on 8 October 1953 in these terms:

The Soviets now possess a stockpile of atomic weapons of conventional types and we must futhermore conclude that the powerful explosion of August 12th last was produced by a weapon, or the forerunner of a weapon, of power far in excess of the conventional types.

We, therefore, conclude that the Soviets now have the capability of atomic attack on us, and such capability will increase with the passage of time.

America's security in the final analysis rests upon the initiative, vision, and unselfish devotion of its citizens. It is a responsibility that cannot be shifted. We and we alone can discharge that responsibility.

Arthur S. Flemming
Director of
Defense Mobilization

Preface

The Industrial College of the Armed Forces was established to prepare selected officers of the Armed Forces, both Regular and Reserve, and civilian executives for important managerial positions in time of emergency. Instruction is provided in three forms: (1) resident, (2) correspondence, and (3) traveling lecture teams. The base for all three types of instruction is the same.

Experience attests to the great value of the correspondence course. The subject matter is presented in small volumes for convenience, each volume representing a major division of the subject. They are reorganized and revised from time to time to bring them up to date and to place emphasis as change may dictate upon those phases of the course deemed most important. Considerable background and illustrative materials are included as a basis for broad and comprehensive education in the field of world resources and their use in support of national objectives.

The texts consist of materials written by members of the faculty of the Industrial College, of selected lectures delivered at the College, and of selections from various publications. The texts in use were prepared mainly by the Correspondence Text Committee of the Education Division of the College. Current revisions of these texts are prepared by the Branches of the Education Division and coordinated by the Committee, which consists of Dr. Benjamin H. Williams, Chairman, Dr. Harold J. Clem, Dr. Louis C. Hunter, Dr. Andrew J. Kress, and Dr. Samuel H. McGuire. Suggestions and recommendations are based on the instructional policy of the Correspondence Study Branch as well as on student reactions to text materials.

The Industrial College owes a debt of gratitude to a number of lecturers, writers, and publishers who have permitted the use of their materials in this series of texts. Specific acknowledgments are made in each volume for these contributions.

This volume, *The Nature of Economic Mobilization*, is adapted by Dr. Hunter from his lectures given at the College, except that chapter III was written by Dr. Benjamin H. Williams.

H. T. DEUTERMANN,
Rear Admiral, USN,
Deputy Commandant,
Extension Courses Division.

11 June 1956

ix

397073°—56——2

Introduction

"Where there is no vision, the people perish."

President Eisenhower stated, "We live in an age of peril."

Ours is an era of rapid change. The weapons, techniques, tactics, and even strategy of today are all too often obsolescent tomorrow. While we must not lose sight of the lessons learned in the recent world war and in Korea, we must stress the "forward look." The profound and continuous changes in the threat facing us these days indicate that survival is much more dependent upon readiness than upon capability for rapid mobilization. Yet complete military preparation to meet all contingencies would entail such prodigious expenditure of manpower and money as to jeopardize our economy. Our aim, therefore, is to create a happy medium between all-out readiness and mobilization as we have practiced it in the past.

This course is a study based on the concept of national readiness for emergency. There are some experts who reason that there will be no time for mobilization in a war of the future. This tenet we hold to be extreme. We must be ready, whatever the nature of the attack, to bring to bear our manpower and industrial capacity to maximum efficiency in the shortest possible time. To monitor this program, an effective and responsive office has been established in the executive department of our Government—the Office of Defense Mobilization.

The problems of combating inflation, balancing the budget, evolving an adequate tax program, maintaining a system of selective service, providing funds for foreign aid, and guarding against a recession are also part and parcel of the overall problems of readiness for emergency management of the National Economy.

Now, as never before in its history, the mission of the Industrial College and its motto might well be made our nation's watchword. "Industria et Defensio Inseparabiles." Certainly the Soviets have shown the world that they well understand the inseparability of Industry and Defense.

Twice within the present century the United States has been forced to go to war for which it was ill-prepared. Our European allies in each instance bore the brunt of the early stages of war. Their lands were overrun, their cities destroyed, their industries ruined, their social and civic activities were disrupted. But this nation escaped those calamities, thanks to the vast ocean space around us and precious time bought by our allies. Technology now has robbed us of those cushions of Time and Space. Our land has long been spared the ravages of invaders and our people have never lived under an alien occupation army. World War I, World War II, and Korea have shown us the cost in effort and money of our traditional aversion to military preparedness. Today the cost might well be failure to survive with our culture. Conversion from a peacetime to a modern war status is not the answer. A responsive readiness for emergency must supersede the conversion premise of tradition.

Boom times breed complacency. We live in an atmosphere of high production, industrial growth, and a rising standard of living. The rosy complexion of life tends to obscure the threat from without. We lean toward a hope that any Soviet change to a policy of affability might reflect a fundamental change in their stated objective of world domination.

The United States peacetime policy of a degree of military preparedness is of only recent adoption. In the past the military forces were kept at a minimum. Today the historic shift from a status of nonpreparedness to one of war would be too great; and the demands on the economy too heavy. Korea may be considered as the turning point in national policy for dealing with a surprise attack. The continuing peril in the world political outlook makes a higher degree of readiness requisite to our survival.

The major economic effort in the United States normally is directed toward increased production in order to provide a higher standard of living for our growing population. Above this any degree of mobilization for national security requires a corresponding increased production. If the threat to national security is great, as in war, it becomes necessary both to curtail consumer goods and to increase total production.

A war economy makes demands upon agriculture, lumbering, fishing, mining, manufacturing, transportation, communications, power, water supply, wholesale and retail distribution, public and private finance, foreign trade, and the entire economy. It involves every phase of human, economic, political, and diplomatic relations. "Mobilization planning in its widest sense is the welding together of broad political, military, economic, and psychological factors, both nationally and internationally . . ."[1] Economic mobilization for national security is used to encompass the organization, direction, and controls necessary in the operation of the national economy in a war emergency or in planning for national defense.

National security is dependent upon a number of vital factors in the economy, among which human resources, natural resources, and productive efficiency are paramount. In an emergency, we will need

---

[1] *Mobilization Planning and the National Security* (1950–1960) *Problems and Issues,* Legislative Reference Service, Library of Congress, Government Printing Office, Washington, 1950.

to establish controls to achieve concurrently the national goals—military success, provision for consumer necessities, and the preservation of national institutions. In the light of the sudden devastation that an enemy can inflict, many actions must be planned in time of peace for instant application upon the outbreak of hostilities or even with positive knowledge that an outbreak is looming.

Industry chews up such vast amounts of many raw materials that it would be difficult, if not impossible, to supply them in wartime. Although we have an abundance of certain materials, we are short of others and must depend upon imports, substitutes, and a program of stockpiling to see that resources are available for war.

War requires production for which sufficient raw materials cannot be quickly provided. If importation of materials is cut off by enemy action, peacetime procedures may fail to cope with the situation. Unrestricted bidding by alarmed manufacturers would play havoc with integrated production plans. Competition between government agencies might be equally disastrous. Under a system of war-alarmed competitive bidding, the prices would skyrocket and economic mobilization would be paralyzed. This is why, in the two World Wars, the belligerents found it necessary to regulate, ration, and allocate raw materials.

We also must take account of our international responsibilities and commitments. The Director of Defense Mobilization emphasized this point in his Second Quarterly Report to the President. "It reports not only on the defense mobilization of the United States but on the progress of building defensive strength throughout the free world." [2] On this point he stated, "but the program of defense mobilization is a free world program—not a national program. Every free nation shares in a common peril, and every free nation must join in a common effort. . . . As we and our partner nations now tackle the difficult problems of controlling and distributing our resources, all of must remember the fundamental fact that the free world is being menaced as a whole and that it must respond as a whole." [3]

The importance then of careful planning to facilitate prompt response to an attack and of deterrent forces to help preclude an attack are evident. We must give consideration during the period of comparative quiet to these problems. Such planning should be kept current and yet be long range.

Major problems of readiness constitute the subject matter of the correspondence course, "*Emergency Management of the National Economy.*" A better understanding of these problems by our citizen-

[2] Wilson, Charles E., "Meeting Defense Goals, a Must for Everyone," July 1, 1951, p. III.
[3] Ibid., pp. 2, 3.

executives should contribute to their effective participation in using our total resources for security. It should make executives in industry and the professions better able to cope with the nonmilitary tasks arising in an emergency.

This course is presented, therefore, and dedicated to a better understanding of the readiness required to survive in this age of peril.

R. P. HOLLIS,
Major General, USA,
Commandant.

CONTENTS

TABLES

FIGURES

I
BASIC TERMS AND CONCEPTS

ECONOMIC MOBILIZATION

Economic mobilization has to do with the supply or logistical side of warfare.

It is the process by which all the productive resources of the economy are organized and directed in support of the Armed Forces, whether for defense or for war. It is concerned with obtaining answers to the basic questions: How do we get the men, the materials, the money, and the munitions with which to fight? How do we get them in the amounts needed, where needed, and when needed for the effective conduct of military operations?

LOGISTICS

The science and conduct of warfare break down into three major divisions: strategy, tactics, and logistics. Strategy determines the overall military objectives and plans for the conduct of the war. Strategy supports the political objectives or goals of the nation. Tactics have to do with the direction and conduct of specific military operations—combat operations. Tactics, in other words, are the methods for attaining the strategic objectives. Logistics has to do with providing the supply base, the material ways and means essential to the successful conduct of tactical operations.

In recent years the term logistics has been given a much broader and more inclusive interpretation than has been customary in the past. The traditional, and narrow, concept of logistics is defined in Webster as "the branch of the military art which embraces the details of the transport, quartering, and supply of troops in military operations."

In this narrow concept of logistics, as it was long used, the production and even the procurement of military supplies was customarily ignored or taken for granted. Logistics was usually thought of as limited to supply operations in the field. In the past twenty years, however, the concept of logistics has been greatly expanded, until it is given a definition so broad as to include the entire industrial and economic base of military operations. Economic mobilization and logistics, however, differ chiefly in point of emphasis. In logistics, attention is frequently fixed on the distribution or field supply; while

1

in economic mobilization, attention is focused upon the resource and production base of military operations.

THE REVOLUTION IN WARFARE

This process which we call economic mobilization is a byproduct of a military revolution that has taken place during the last generation. On the surface it appears to be the result of new military weapons and new military techniques, and of the application of science and technology to warfare. It is obvious, of course, that it is made possible by scientific research and development; but the causes go even deeper. In a broader sense it rests upon the tremendous increases in productive resources and productive capacity which have taken place in the world during the past 75 years, chiefly in Western Europe, the United States, and in the Asiatic world, Japan. This new kind of warfare has been in active preparation about the same length of time, but it is only since 1939 that we have come to understand its full implications and to realize its full possibilities.

Some features of this revolution in warfare are easy to see and, in a way, to understand. Devices such as rockets, proximity fuses, atomic bombs, jet propulsion, and radar are as spectacular as they are effective. Any one of us can grasp their importance quickly enough. For this reason the significance of science and technology in war is widely appreciated, even if it is not very well understood by most of us. The key role of manufacturing in warfare is also widely recognized. Production lines turning out tanks instead of locomotives, aircraft instead of automobiles, radar instead of radios, and guns instead of washing machines are aspects of a war effort which all can comprehend. No phase of our recent war effort, apart from the strictly military phase, received more publicity. After all, the production phase was the one through which most civilians had their most direct contact with the war.

Other aspects of this military revolution are much less well known and much less understood. This is especially true of the economic aspect and of the organizational and administrative aspects of war. To most people the economic system, even in its normal operations, is a considerable mystery; to grasp the workings of a complicated war economy is likewise baffling. It is with these nonmilitary and non-scientific aspects of modern war that we are here chiefly concerned.

THE PART OF THE CIVILIAN

Combat is no longer, as it has been for centuries, the principal part of warfare. This is a view that many, both in the military profession and outside, will be reluctant to accept. It runs contrary to long tradition and experience. To put it a little differently, warfare is no longer, as it was for centuries, principally the business of the military. The civilian side of war has come in many respects to overshadow the strictly military side. Even within the armed services a large proportion of the personnel are engaged in duties which are mainly civilian in character, such as procurement and various supply matters behind the front lines. Behind every man in uniform there are several civilians—men and women—engaged in activities essential to keep the military forces in the field. These persons give their time, labor, and, in areas within enemy bombing range such as the European and Far Eastern theaters in the last war, often give their lives in the war effort. In fact, the traditional distinction between military and civilian is coming to have less and less meaning in wartime. It is quite probable that in the next war it will have no meaning at all.

The military strength and capabilities of nations can no longer be measured solely or even primarily in terms of the size of the armed forces, the bravery and fighting spirit of the common soldier and the skill of military leaders in the strategy and tactics of war. Modern war has, in fact, become a struggle in which the entire resources of nations are pitted against each other. It is a struggle not only between the productive resources such as mills and factories of the belligerent powers; but is also a struggle between the economies of the nations involved through which these resources are made effective for war purpoes.

More than that, modern war has become a contest also between the governmental institutions, the organizational systems, and the administrative techniques and procedures necessary to mobilize the economic resources of the nation for war. In fact, in the science and practice of modern war, a sound economic principle or a new and effective administrative practice may be fully as important as, or even of greater importance than, a new weapon or the outcome of a major combat action.

THE LOGISTICAL PYRAMID

The relationships of the major elements which contribute to the military power of a nation are suggested by the analogy of a pyramid which has been termed a "logistical pyramid" (figure 1). At the apex of the pyramid are the Armed Forces. These may be termed the spearhead, the cutting edge of the national war machine. Under them lies the vast economic potential of the country. In the layer immediately below the apex is what might be called the industrial support or backup of the Armed Forces. It includes the great number and variety of manufacturing industries engaged in the production of what are termed military end items—the thousands of articles of military equipment and supply from tanks to toothbrushes, from aircraft to armored vehicles, from clothing to cannon, from food to fuel—used and consumed directly by the Armed Forces. It includes endless civilian type articles as well as munitions in the strictly military sense of the term. This layer is made up of tens of thousands of industrial facilities and business organizations; the prime contractors, the sub-contractors, the "sub-subs" and the suppliers of all of these in turn.

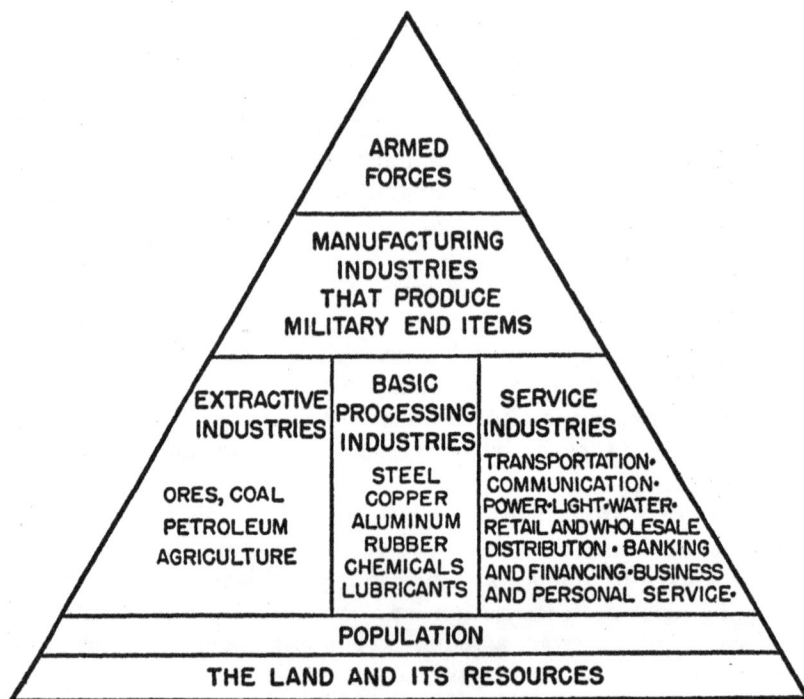

Figure 1. The logistical pyramid.

However crucial are the operations of these thousands of manufacturing concerns for the equipment and logistical support of the Armed Forces, it is obvious that manufacturing industries producing the end items do not stand alone. They are dependent in turn upon a wide variety of supporting industries and services. Beneath the layer of manufacturing industries there is placed another layer which is in many respects broader and deeper than the industrial layer above. This third layer in the logistical pyramid is divided into three major parts, representing the extractive industries, the basic precessing in- dustries and the service industries. The extractive industries are the primary industries which supply the raw material needs of the nation: the metallic ores and nonmetallic minerals; the fuels, such as coal, petroleum and natural gas; the wide range of agricultural products, both food products and industrial raw materials; and the many products of the forest industries.   The basic processing industries include industries of such critical importance as steel, copper, aluminum, and a long list of other nonferrous and special alloy metals, as well as the heavy chemicals, petroleum products, synthetic rubber, and plastics. Then comes a whole cluster of what, for want of a better term, are called the service industries.   These include the great transportation systems of the country; railroads and steamships, truck and bus lines, air transport lines, pipelines, inland waterways.   Closely related are the communication systems; the postal service, telegraph and telephone services, radio broadcasting, the newspapers and periodicals—to list only the most important.   This layer includes, too, the great utility services, supplying power, light, water, and waste disposal.   Finally, there are the wide variety of business services which play so vital a role in the economic system: banking, financial and insurance services, the produce and stock exchanges, the elaborate systems of wholesale and retail distribution of goods, advertising, and many others.

At the bottom of this logistical pyramid are two broad layers on which the entire pyramid rests, the *population base*, which plays so fundamental a role in the economy whether in peace or war, and the *land* itself, with its soil and subsoil resources, its geographic features and its climate.   This concept of the logistical pyramid obviously oversimplifies greatly the actual situation.   For example, it fails to indicate the close interdependence of the various layers and their several components.   Clearly, the service industries depend upon the manufacturing and extractive industries, and the extractive upon the manufacturing and service industries, and so on.   Yet, while the chart does oversimplify the situation, it is useful in suggesting how deeply rooted is the military strength of the modern nation.   A failure in any major part of this pyramidal structure will be felt, sooner or later, in a slowing down or reduction in size of the stream of supplies and munitions which is the life-blood of the armed forces.   A crop failure, a transportation breakdown, a power shortage, a major strike—any one of these can have serious military consequences.   Strike at the foundations, at the roots of military power, and you weaken that power. These are commonplace but fundamental facts in the experience of our generation, but they are relatively new in the history of organized warfare.   And there are many today, among both civilians and the military, who have not fully grasped their significance, although the experience of World War II and the postwar defense emergency has greatly reduced the area of ignorance and misunderstanding.

MOBILIZATION: INDUSTRIAL AND ECONOMIC

With these factors in mind, the significance of the terms "industrial mobilization" and "economic mobilization" becomes apparent. These terms are simply adaptations of the much older expression, "military mobilization." Military mobilization in the traditional usage refers to the process by which, on the eve of war, military units in reserve are called up for service, equipped, and assembled in organized bodies. The tremendous and quite unforeseen demands for munitions in the early part of World War I called attention to the vital role of the industries which supplied these munitions. The traditional methods of procurement of these supplies were found inadequate to provide the amounts needed with the speed essential for the support of the military actions in progress. Sweeping measures by the Government were found necessary to remove the obstacles to the attainment of production and procurement goals. In a very real sense, industry came to be "mobilized" no less than the military forces themselves, although in a different manner; that is, the munitions and supporting industries and services were organized, directed, and controlled to the end of obtaining greatly increased output of munitions. Manufacturers, for example, were told what they could and what they could not produce. Scarce raw and semi-finished materials were allowed only to producers of essential war goods; prices were placed under controls; scarce consumer goods were rationed, and so on. Other economic activities than industry felt the impact of tremendous wartime demands; but the principal bottleneck, or the bottleneck most readily perceived and understood, was in the industries manufacturing munitions. The phrase, "industrial mobilization," was coined to describe and to emphasize the process of preparing and controlling industry in order to meet the unprecedentedly great demands of modern war for munitions and military supplies of all kinds.

The concept of industrial mobilization, an outgrowth of World War I experience, proved very useful in the postwar years of the 1920's and 1930's. It drove home the lesson that it takes more than armies, navies, and air forces to fight modern wars. It emphasized the importance of planning and preparedness for the industrial base no less than for the military forces which engage in combat. World War II brought into use the broader and more inclusive concept of "economic mobilization" which recognized that not only manufacturing industry but all the economic resources of the nation must be organized and directed in support of the Armed Forces. That means, to refer to figure 1 showing the logistical pyramid, that the economic activities indicated in the lower layers of the pyramid all must be mobilized to the extent necessary and in the manner necessary to insure maximum production at the level of manufacturing industries.

THE PRODUCTION SYSTEM AS THE FOUNDATION OF MILITARY EFFORT

In any age, the conduct of war requires certain essentials, beginning with men—manpower—withdrawn from civilian occupations to fill the armies and to man the ships. These men must be clothed, fed, and given some kind of shelter and medical care. They must be equipped with weapons and supplied with ammunition, whether rocks, arrows, bullets, or bombs. They must be transported to wherever needed in support of tactical operations or strategic plans; in earlier ages by leg power or horse power; in recent years by steam or electric power, or by the internal combustion engine. As the size of armies and navies has increased, the problems of logistics become both larger and more complex as the organizational and administrative tasks multiply.

Where are all the materials, men, and munitions obtained with which to supply the operations of the Armed Forces in field and at sea? Under the simpler conditions of warfare in earlier times, fighting men often brought their own equipment and supplies or lived off the country to a considerable extent. Under conditions of organized warfare, involving substantial bodies of men operating for extended periods, supply problems are the responsibility of the government which conducts the military operations. In the last analysis, however, men, equipment, and supplies have to be obtained from the productive resources of the nation, from field and factory, from mine and mill, from the manpower and material wealth of the nation.

Collectively these productive resources, supplemented and supported by transportation and power, banking and finance, wholesale and retail distribution, and all the numerous and often elaborate institutions of business and exchange, constitute the economy or the economic system. The economic system is a framework within the limits of which military operations, so far as scale and intensity are concerned, are confined. It is the foundation upon which military strength rests. Sometimes, it is true, an invading army can maintain itself to a considerable extent upon food and supplies seized in the enemy country. In this case the productive resources of the latter simply serve to enlarge those of the invading power. History provides many examples of this practice, from the invasions of Europe by the "barbarian hordes" down to the exploitation of conquered areas by Germany and Japan in World War II.

The material requirements of the Armed Forces must be supplied by the economic system and are limited by the productive capacity of this system. The extent and duration of military operations, the size of armies, navies, and air forces, and the types of weapons, equipment, and other supplies are all dependent on the kind of economic system and the type and quantity of its production. The study of economic mobilization, therefore, has its origin in the study of the productive system which is the foundation of all military effort.

Since, in the physical sense, war is waged with the four M's—men, materials, munitions, and money—its relation to the prevailing economic system is always fundamental. Other things being equal, the ability of a nation to wage war depends on the ability of its economy to produce a *surplus of goods* beyond the requirements of the civilian population—a surplus which can be devoted to the support and maintenance of armed forces. The greater the productive efficiency of the economy; i. e., the system of production as outlined in the logistical pyramid, the higher the level at which the economy operates; and the more advanced the technology available for use in production and combat, the greater is the scale, intensity, and duration of military operations which a nation or society is capable of supporting.

The actual process of mobilizing economic resources in support of warfare, of course, varies with the nature of the warfare and with the character of the economic system. It varies with the kind and efficiency of production. In a simple agricultural economy, based on small farms, hand tools, and a minimum of trade, economic mobilization is one thing; in a highly industrialized economy, employing a high degree of specialization, machine production, and an elaborate system of distribution and exchange, it is quite a different thing. The problems of raising, equipping, and supplying armed forces have changed not only in response to new conditions of technology and new methods of production but as a consequence of changes in government and social organization. The economic problems of modern warfare are, in particular, radically different from those characteristic of earlier periods, and they are best understood if seen against the background of the past.

II
LOGISTICAL CHARACTERISTICS OF HISTORIC PERIODS

FEUDALISM

The feudal regime of Western Europe in the Middle Ages contrasts sharply with the structure of modern capitalist society. Feudal conditions were in some respects very favorable to war. There was no strong central authority to compel order and to repress warfare among the nobility. An agricultural economy of almost primitive simplicity provided little outlet for the energies and ambitions of the landed aristocracy, save in territorial and personal aggrandizement.

On the other hand, economic and technological conditions prevented the resulting strife from rising much above the level of local, desultory, and short-lived warfare. An inefficient, self-sufficient agricultural economy, lacking specialized manufacturing and with almost no trade, was barely able to supply an undernourished population with its minimum physical requirements. Such a production system could not provide the surplus wealth necessary to support military conflict on anything more than a very petty scale. Warfare was largely a monopoly of a small leisure class, the higher nobility, aided by the lesser gentry under obligation to provide military service, customarily limited to forty days or less each year. The meager resources of the nobility, the difficulties of transportation and travel, and the heavy cost of equipment in horses and armor confined warfare not only to a few people but also to brief periods, and drastically limited the radius of military operations. The urge to mutual annihilation was sharply checked by the hard facts of economic conditions.

EARLY NATIONALISM

The economic and social bases of war underwent significant changes in the centuries which marked the transition from the medieval to the modern period. These changes were reflected in the social role of war and in the organization and conduct of warfare. The centralization of political authority in the national state, the growth of rich and extensive overseas empires, the development of parliamentary government, the expansion of trade and commerce, and the rise of the middle class all had important consequences for war. Of particular significance was the growth of internal commerce and of international trade. Western society emerged from the medieval economy, based on a crude and self-sufficient agriculture, developing a regional and con-

9

tinental specialization and interchange of goods. The resulting increase of productive efficiency created a mounting surplus of labor and goods, and concentrated increasingly in the hands of a growing middle class of merchants, bankers, and other business men, a supply of wealth which under favorable conditions could be and was diverted to the purpose of war.

In contrast with the feudal era, when wealth was chiefly in the form of land and buildings which could with difficulty be converted to military ends, the surplus wealth of the capitalist economy was concentrated especially in money and movable goods. This wealth, when tapped by rulers through taxation and loans, was readily applied to the support of armies. Moreover, the new world disclosed by overseas discoveries rich rewards in resources and markets to those nations able to seize and exploit them. This wealth in turn made possible and even required the support of still larger armed forces for the protection and enlargement of empire. The aggressive forces of nationalism and capitalism thus gave mutual support to each other and provided new and broader bases for war.

The military counterparts of the new political and economic system were the professional standing armies and navies which first appeared in the sixteenth and seventeenth centuries. Improvements in the weapons of war, due to the use of gunpowder and increased mobility resulting from improved roads and better ships and navigation methods, led to military operations on a scale rarely approached in the earlier centuries. Under the spur of national crises, the war-making capabilities of the new economic and political system were demonstrated further during the period of the French Revolution. Under the stress of a revolutionary situation, the principle of the *levee en masse*—the arming of all able-bodied men—was successfully adopted and became a fixed institution among the major Continental powers. So far as manpower was concerned, the concept of total war was beginning to take form. During the Napoleonic era, great armies marched, counter-marched, and battled from one end of Europe to the other. War was conducted on a scale and with an intensity hitherto unknown, and, with interruptions of varying length, it was waged for periods of many years. The problem of equipping and supplying such forces and operations taxed the financial and industrial resources of the nations involved. The maneuvers and spectacular clashes of the opposing armies have tended to monopolize the attention of students of this warfare; but to the governments involved, the crucial issues were of securing the men, the money, and the munitions required to support such tremendous and such sustained military operations.

THE AMERICAN FRONTIER PERIOD

It is unnecessary to depend on European experience for illustrations of the manner in which warfare has been related to changing economic, social, and technological conditions. In the course of a relatively brief span of time, America has evolved through many stages of economic development. In less than a century a large part of our country has passed from the near primitive conditions of a self-sufficient frontier society to the highly specialized and intricate industrialism of the present generation. Throughout our national experience and reaching back to the earliest colonial beginnings, war has run an intermittent course. The interactions and relationships between warfare and economic life have been in consequence as varied as the evolutionary stages through which the American economy has passed.

Economic and social conditions in the typical frontier region of the colonial period were even more primitive in some respects than those which characterized feudal society in the Middle Ages. Defensive and offensive operations against the Indians were closely interwoven with the making of a living and the everyday life and habits of the people. A frontier society was compelled to maintain a constant state of mobilization of men and material resources under penalty of death or torture for the luckless individual, and of extinction for the community that was unprepared. The concentration of homes in a compact settlement was an essential measure of defense. Powder, lead, and salt were the strategic materials of these often bloody times; guns, axes, knives, and shot-mould the equipment of war. Fertile lands were both the objects of strife and the bases of military and economic strength. Muskets were as essential for the cultivation of fields as plow or hoe. When periodically the storm of conflict broke, the entire manpower of the settlement, men and women, young and old, each performing the duties appropriate to age and condition, fought off the savage foe from the shelter of community blockhouse or barricaded homes. The fact of total mobilization was as familiar as the phrase was unknown. The maintenance of the community's resources in a state of readiness for war was a common condition of survival.

Sporadic warfare was waged on the American frontier with the Indians, not only during the seventeenth and eighteenth centuries, but in some parts of the country well into the middle of the nineteenth century. Lacking other protection, isolated frontier settlements were compelled to defend themselves as best they could. They were dependent on themselves, not only for fighting men, but for most of the supplies and equipment to support these men.

The economic basis for this frontier warfare was of a primitive kind: an inefficient subsistence economy in which every family made its living directly from the soil, producing little beyond the bare necessities of food, clothing, shelter, and the simplest of household and farm tools and utensils. Each frontiersman had his own arsenal—musket or rifle, hunting knife, powder horn and shot bag—and was his own quartermaster, providing and taking with him a bag of meal and jerked meat for food, with perhaps a little salt, and using shanks' mare for transport. Under such conditions military and economic mobilization were hardly to be distinguished. In the struggle, literally for survival, each community mobilized all its resources, human and material, against the savage enemy. Its action had to be prompt and direct; the means for defense and, on occasion, for offensive forays had to be ready at all times.

THE REVOLUTIONARY WAR

Warfare in the formal sense, involving the entire nation in armed conflict with another power, posed quite different problems. In studying the War for Independence, for example, we are struck with the great difficulty met in mobilizing even a small fraction of the resources of the colonies. This was in part due to the fact that the colonists were themselves divided. An influential minority stood in active opposition to revolution, and another substantial part of the population lent no active support to the colonial cause. More important were factors inherent in the colonial economy. The conditions controlling the organization and conduct of warfare on a countrywide basis prevented anything approaching a full realization of the potentialities for war exhibited in the local defense of frontier communities. National warfare called for raising, equipping, supplying, and moving large bodies of troops against the concentrated forces of the enemy, which were attempting to seize and control the focal points of colonial economic life, the seaports. Since the colonial economy was predominantly agricultural, with fully nine-tenths of the people making a living directly from the land, it was with great difficulty that the necessary equipment, supplies, and soldiers could be obtained. Because of inadequate transportation and the lack of markets, most of the population produced simply for their own needs, growing and making nearly everything they consumed and used. This inefficient subsistence economy could produce but a small surplus to be devoted to the wasteful and destructive business of war.

Accustomed as the colonies were to obtaining substantial quantities of manufactures from England, the breaking of relations confronted them with the necessity of meeting both the normal needs of the civilian population and the heavy requirements of the Army from the limited resources of domestic manufacturing. The numerous efforts to encourage domestic manufacturing which accompanied the nonimportation agreements in the controversy preceding the outbreak of war aided the colonies in making the transition to a war economy, but did not meet such specific military demands as munitions. Since manufacturing was conducted on a handicraft and country mill basis, the procurement of the large quantities of clothing, shoes, blankets, and other equipment required by the Army presented serious problems. Many supplies were imported in spite of the British blockade, but the difficulties of transport hampered their distribution to points of need. Four months after a much needed shipment of clothing was received at Portsmouth, some of the lot had not left the town, and none had been moved farther than Springfield, some 150 miles away. The war was fought largely by foot soldiers and every farmer had his own musket or rifle. Since engagements were infrequent and fire power low, the requirements for powder and shot were not heavy. Yet, with the very limited resources of the colonies, problems of procurement and production were difficult.

Far more serious were the difficulties of feeding the Army. This phase of the supply story is marked by a series of crises provoked by food scarcity which reduced the Army again and again to one-half, one-quarter, and even one-eighth rations for weeks at a time and threatened the disintegration of the colonial cause from mutiny and rebellion. Because of the self-sufficient character of agriculture, surpluses were small and widely dispersed. Their concentration at points of need was hampered by the difficulties and costs of transportation and by enemy control of the principal channels of commerce. The wretched state of the roads narrowly limited the extent of territory from which supplies could be drawn, and in the rainy seasons of the year movement of supplies was virtually stopped. Conditions of feast and famine were often separated by fifty miles or less. Valley Forge was only twenty miles from Philadelphia.

The difficulties met in supplying the Army were, however, due not as much to the exhaustion of the resources of the colonies as to the inability of the Government to mobilize effectively the available resources through an efficient system of procurement and supply. The Continental Congress, loosely organized and with the feeblest of powers, was reluctant to delegate such authority as it had. Attempting to operate in an administrative as well as a legislative capacity, Congress dealt with the problems of supply through a number of special committees on such matters as muskets, cannon, saltpeter, clothing, and beef. Under the compulsion of events, these committees, which rarely had authority to do more than investigate and report, were replaced by standing committees, and these in turn by boards with somewhat greater powers. It was not until the last phase of the war that Congress was reluctantly brought to adopt departments headed by single administrators.

In the absence of an adequate military procurement organization, much of the purchasing of supplies was handled through private purchasing agents, commonly business men operating as individuals and with but limited financial resources. Merchants engaged in the importing business were frequently commissioned to buy weapons and other supplies wherever they might be found in Europe.

Competition between the agents of state and general governments for limited supplies added to a confusion that at times approached chaos. Financial weakness, due to the lack of taxing power and the uncertainty of the colonial cause, frequently compelled reliance on the cumbersome device of direct contributions of goods by the states, and led early to the resort to paper currency. Printing press finance produced a progressive inflation of the currency, which discredited the colonial cause and created almost insuperable problems in procurement.

Manpower also presented great difficulties. Indifference to the revolutionary cause on the part of many was, of course, an important factor, but more fundamental was the absence of a labor surplus. The struggle to wrest a livelihood from a resistant nature with the crudest of tools and implements left little unused time to be placed at the disposal of the colonial cause. The colonies lived too close to the margin of subsistence to have much to spare in manpower and materials for the prosecution of the war. This was reflected not only in the small size of the armies but even more in the common three month's term of enlistment and the high rate of turnover. Men could not be spared long from their families, especially during the active seasons of farming. During the winter months when farmers had time on their hands, military operations were usually suspended because of the weather.

THE CIVIL WAR

The Civil War, second of the major wars in which this country has been involved, presents a striking example of the close relationships between economic strength and military power. This war was not simply a struggle between the opposing governments and the armed forces which each mobilized against the other. It was a struggle in which the economic systems and resources of the two sides played a vital and decisive role. In years immediately following the achievement of national independence, there was no very great difference between the Northern and Southern states with respect to size of population, total wealth, or the general character of the economic life. In the 75 years between the American Revolution and the Civil War, however, the American economy as a whole underwent very important changes. The population of the United States increased tenfold and the wealth of the nation approximately twenty times. Of special importance during these years was the steady advance of industrialization, with its emphasis upon factory production, the use of machines, mechanical power, and the metal and metal-working industries. The growth of manufacturing industry was accompanied and assisted by a revolution in transportation through the introduction and extension, first of steam navigation on the inland waterways, and, in the 1840's and 1850's, of railroads.

These developments had obviously great meaning for the conduct of warfare. The productive efficiency of the economic system had steadily risen and the surplus of goods, over and above the bare subsistence needs of the population, likewise underwent a substantial increase. This, in turn, made it possible to raise, equip, and support armed forces on a larger scale, proportionately, than during the American Revolution.

This great increase in economic potential and the technology of industrialism brought significant changes both in the conduct of military operations and in strategical objectives. In the weapons of the war there was less change than might be expected. Infantry and cavalry moved into battle with arms which might have been (and in some instances were!) inherited from the armies of the Revolution. Official conservatism so delayed the adoption of the repeating rifle, with its great advantage in fire power over converted flintlocks and muzzle-loading rifles, that its role in the war was negligible, and the opportunity presented for capitalizing the superior industrial resources of the North was, in this instance, lost. Artillery responded more adequately to the new conditions with bigger and better guns employed in greater proportions than hitherto, and naval warfare entered a new era with the introduction of armor plate.

The most important innovations related not to weapons or tactics but to strategy and supply. On the one hand there was a growing recognition of the importance of weakening the enemy by cutting off or destroying the economic bases of his military strength. A major strategical objective of the Federal Government was the isolation and conquest of large productive areas within the Confederacy and the capture and destruction or utilization of railroad centers and lines, mills and factories, cotton, livestock, and other goods. Sherman's army in its march to the sea laid waste the countryside with devastating effectiveness. On the other hand an unprecedented degree of mobility was introduced in warfare. Troops and equipment were moved and supplied on a large scale with extraordinary facility. Whole armies were moved bodily to the scene of battle hundreds of miles distant in a few days and were transferred from one theater to another with hardly less ease. The reason was steam power. Railroads and steamboats, by this time fully integrated in the economy of the nation, were employed on a large scale in the prosecution of the war, not only in the functioning of the civilian economy but in the direct service of the armies—the first such use in a major war in history. Troops, supplies, munitions, and equipment were carried into the heart of the enemy country by steam transportation, permitting the establishment of supply bases close to the scene of battle. The area of dependence on wagon trains was greatly narrowed and the ability to keep armies in the field was materially enhanced by railroads and steamboats. To capture and destroy the rail lines serving the enemy, to sink his boats, and to establish control over rivers as well as coastal waters became major military objectives.

While the nation as a whole had greatly increased its economic potential, that is, its productive capacity, it was divided very unequally between the two belligerent sections. The North, since the Revolutionary War, had moved far ahead of the South in population and in wealth, in transportation facilities and service, in shipping and foreign trade, and, above all, in industrial facilities and capacity of all kinds. Even in agriculture the South lagged behind. In 1860 the hay product of the North exceeded in value all the leading Southern staples combined—cotton, tobacco, rice, and sugar.

Because of this economic superiority, the North was able to raise and support its large armies and navies without great difficulty. In the first year of the war there was much confusion and disorder, for in the North, as in the South, the war was begun quite without plans and preparations. The equipping and supplying of the Federal Armed Forces thereafter was simply a large-scale procurement job, with all the difficulties of that job, and it never went beyond that. In the North, the normal peacetime economic life went on about as usual. Industrial and agricultural expansion, which had been so rapid the generation before the Civil War, proceeded with little check during the war. Throughout the conflict there were few scarcities of any importance and little hardship among civilians, although price inflation bore unequally on different groups. There was no economic or even industrial mobilization, in the proper sense of the term, in the North. There was almost nothing of the central planning and directing which marks the true war economy. No controls were established over resources, production, prices, and, except for the draft, labor.

The Government was authorized in 1862 to take over the railroad and telegraph systems, but, except in the war zone, it did not do so.

The position of the Confederacy was very different and far more difficult. The Southern economy centered in the production of a few staple crops—tobacco, cotton, sugar, and rice—chiefly for foreign markets. The loss of the foreign markets because of the Northern naval blockade was a very serious blow for the South. The Southern states were heavily dependent for manufactured goods upon imports from the North and from England. Both of these sources of supplies were cut off, along with the markets for staple products. The South had almost no heavy industry and was deficient even in such items as textiles, clothing, shoes, and leather goods. At the outset of the war it had no munitions plants. Not only were its transport facilities far inferior to those of the North, but, for lack of replacements of rails, rolling stock, and locomotives, its railroads steadily deteriorated during the course of the war. The result was that the Confederacy found it increasingly difficult to move and supply its armies in the field, and to concentrate in the areas of military operations the supplies drawn from all parts of the Confederacy.

The supply problems of the Confederacy were not primarily in the field of munitions; its military position was never seriously threatened by a lack of small arms, powder, and shot. Shortages in field artillery and munitions at times did definitely handicap the Confederate armies. It was fortunate for the Confederacy that the reliance of both sides during the war was on hand weapons of a simple, not to say antiquated, construction; for, if the weapons of the war had been of a more complicated kind, the industrial North would have had the South at an even greater disadvantage. The really serious problems of war production and supply centered in such commonplace items as clothing, shoes, harness, rails, locomotives, rolling stock, and the like. Two of the most serious shortages, surprisingly enough, which gave the South the most difficulty, were the shortages of horses and salt; and the most critical shortage of all, perhaps, was not in material but in manpower.

It is obvious that the outcome of the Civil War was not determined solely by economic considerations but, to the extent that these considerations were effective, one thing seems clear—because of its limited resources, the South could only expect to win if it used those resources with maximum effectiveness. The Confederacy, in fact, found itself in a situation which really called for an economy directed and controlled by the central government. In order to overcome its economic weaknesses, an effective mobilization of its resources was essential. There were, however, numerous and very serious obstacles to such a mobilization. There was no experience in this country, or elsewhere, to provide guidance in such a mobilization of economic resources. The Confederacy did not have the strong centralized administration required to make such a mobilization effective. Moreover, it had to improvise its central government at the outset, resulting in rough going for the whole wartime job. Also, Southern leaders were opposed to a strong central government on principle. That was a major reason for their secession from the Union—they did not like a strong central government. Throughout the war there was much bickering between the state governments and the Confederate government over the distribution of authority and control between them.

In spite of the difficulties, the Confederate government did take some measures to mobilize its economic resources in support of the military effort. It was done under pressure of urgent necessity. It was not a matter of conscious planning. It was not a matter of a deliberate consideration of all that was involved. These measures, however, represent the beginning of a controlled and directed war economy.

They included, principally, the establishment and operation by the Confederate government of plants for the manufacture of a variety of supplies in the South: clothing, shoes, small arms, artillery, salt, powder, transportation equipment, and so on. They included, too, the setting up of certain controls over transportation, chiefly the railroads. The Confederate government established certain limited controls over manpower and materials, operating chiefly through the draft and draft exemptions and through transportation priorities of a very crude kind. It exercised rather close control over foreign trade, including government operation of blockade runners. There were even controls over agriculture, chiefly restrictions on cotton and tobacco planting, which many pertinacious planters continued to produce, although these crops were of no use whatever, but rather a hindrance, in the war effort.

In terms of the things that the Confederate government tried to do, the record is rather impressive; but this effort to mobilize economic resources had only a very limited success. The effort finally failed, and at last the Southern economy almost literally broke down. The Confederacy lost the war not so much on the battlefields as on the economic and administrative fronts.

The experience of the Confederacy is interesting because the South in important respects was closer to total war than anything we experienced in this country during either of two World Wars. For example, substantially the entire white male population of military age, not exempted by law, was enrolled in the Army, amounting to an equivalent of three years service from over a million men out of a total white population of 5.5 million. So far as the civilian population was concerned, nothing in the two World Wars in this country can compare with the hardships and privation suffered in the Confederacy. In view of the striking differences in the material resources of the contestants, the ability of the South to continue the war so long was remarkable.

WORLD WAR I

Between the collapse of the Confederacy and the outbreak of the First World War in 1914, a period of 50 years, many economic changes took place in this country. These transformations were largely a continuation of the developments which had their origin in the first half of the century. Population expanded many times, industrialization advanced rapidly, and there were great advances in mechanization in all branches of economic life. New materials, such as steel, petroleum, and rubber, came to play an important role. The chemical industries rose to a position of industrial prominence, and new sources of power, such as the electric motor and the internal combustion engine, came into wide use.

The economic results of this widespread industrialization were very great. The total national wealth of the United States increased several times as rapidly as the population. The surplus income beyond the bedrock requirements of the civilian population and available for the support of warfare showed an even greater increase.

Other equally significant results of the great advances in productive efficiency and in technology were the new types of weapons and other military equipment which these developments made possible. These new weapons in turn provided the basis for a new kind of warfare. The key to this new warfare can be summed up in two phrases—the mechanization of combat and the industrialization of supply.

As pointed out earlier, a beginning in the industrialization of supply was made during the Civil War, but with minor exceptions, actual combat in the Civil War, as in the Revolutionary War, had been mainly a hand operation employing hand weapons. By the time of the First World War, combat itself had become mechanized to an important degree as the result of the development and introduction of important new weapons: the breech-loading rifle using the metallic cartridge, the machine gun, the rapid-fire field gun. Similiar advances had been made in the mechanization of naval weapons and, above all, in the evolution of the warship from sail to steam, and the introduction of the submarine. Combat was mechanized further by the introduction of the airplane and the tank, both made possible by the internal combustion engine; and the motor truck and automobile in turn advanced mechanization in transport and supply into the combat areas.

By 1914, the ground had been prepared for warfare on a scale and with an intensity that were unprecedented. Huge conscript armies of millions of men were mobilized and put in the field. The early attempts of Germany to force a quick decision were defeated, and there followed the long stalemate of trench warfare on fronts hundreds of miles long. The large numbers engaged, the long sustained actions, and the high rate of fire power produced enormous expenditures of ammunition and other supplies. For example, in the preliminary bombardment in 1917 in the third battle of Ypres, 2,300 guns on a fifteen-mile front expended over 100,000 tons of shells. The average weekly expenditure of shells by the British in France rose from 2,000 tons at the end of 1915 to over 100,000 tons at the end of the war. Naval warfare was much less intensive, but submarines took a very heavy toll of shipping and supplies.

The scale of the supply problem resulting from these conditions exceeded by far anything that had been anticipated by any of the belligerent powers. The struggle soon settled down into an endurance contest in which the outcome, it became clear, would depend largely on the ability of the belligerents to meet the very heavy drain on their productive resources. The main burden of the war of attrition fell upon the industries supplying the munitions requirements of the armed forces, but, before long, scarcities of food, raw materials, general industrial capacity, and manpower appeared. Supply crises in one form or another developed within all the belligerent powers and threatened the success of military operations.

Under the compulsion of these conditions, the governments found themselves compelled to take extraordinary measures, and they established direct controls over their economies at critical points: control over scarce materials in order to channel them into war production; control over foodstuffs through rationing; control over prices, profits, and credit; control over transport facilities, manpower, and so on.

These controls were established only gradually and in a piecemeal fashion, as the pressure of events compelled the governments to act. They changed radically the operation of the economic systems of the belligerent powers. In this manner the war economy was born.

When the United States entered the war, in April 1917, the position of the Allies was critical. They were approaching the limits of their resources in materials, manpower, and productive capacity, just as many months earlier they had nearly exhausted their credit for purchases in the United States. We brought to the Allies the greatest industrial capacity of any nation in the world, but it was capacity geared almost entirely to the production of civilian type goods for civilian needs. The first and most critical problem faced was that of converting this industrial power into military power, and quickly.

Yet, with all our productive skill and with the best will in the world, under the pressure of the urgent war situation, from 12 to 20 months were required to get into production the more critical items of munitions, such as artillery, planes, and machine guns. And there was much reluctance on the part of many manufacturers to convert to war production.

A second major problem appeared at an early stage, just as it appeared in the European countries—scarcities in basic metals, lumber, foodstuffs, fuel, and heavy chemicals. Productive capacity could be increased only slowly. Our priorities systems had to be devised and operated to channel scarce materials to places where they were most needed and not simply where they commanded the highest prices.

A third major problem was a transportation bottleneck which retarded both industrial and military aspects of the war effort. On top of a great increase in domestic transport requirements, resulting from expansion of production, was added the huge job of transporting an army of two million men to Europe and of keeping them supplied. This, plus heavy shipments of Allied supplies and the heavy toll taken of ships by submarine warfare, required our building up merchant tonnage on a large scale. Expansion of shipbuilding facilities became necessary. Rail transport broke down under the load of wartime demands, and the Federal Government took over the operation of the railroads for the duration.

Other major problems centered in the labor and price fields. Price inflation presented the more serious of the two problems. The objective was not simply one of maintaining price stability to minimize disturbances to business operations; it was also one of keeping down the cost of war and of keeping up public morale.

Finally, there was the problem of overall coordination of the war production effort.

All these problems and many lesser ones were, of course, not separate and distinct problems. They were all interrelated and interdependent. No one could be solved simply by itself. Moreover, the many different production programs had to be kept in balance with each other. There must not be too much ammunition and a lack of guns to use it. Unless we had the necessary shipping to get the supplies to Europe, what was the use of manufacturing the supplies? Somebody had to sit on top and direct the many phases of the economic mobilization effort, for, without such overall coordination, the whole war effort might bog down.

When the United States entered the war, the military authorities and a few civilians had some general idea, at least, of the immense job which had to be done, as the result of their observation of developments in the European war.   But we were almost completely lacking in plans for doing the job.   There was little conception, for example, either of the requirements for everything from end items to raw materials, or of the industrial capacity and output to meet those requirements.   There was little general awareness of the need for central direction and control of war production.   It was necessary to develop an elaborate system of war agencies to direct the various phases of the mobilization effort; but this was done reluctantly, slowly, and by a series of improvisations and makeshifts.   In fact, by the time the organizational machinery for the direction of the war production effort was fairly complete, the war was practically over.

The most important of these war agencies was the War Industries Board, set up in July 1917 to replace an advisory commission established some months earlier.   The effectiveness of the War Industries Board, however, was limited by the lack of any real authority over production until March 1918.   The passage of the Overman Act at this time gave priority and other powers to the President, and he delegated much of this power to the Chairman of the War Industries Board, Bernard Baruch.   Under Baruch as Chairman, the War Industries Board served as a kind of industrial general staff for the direction and coordination of efforts on the economic front of the war. It was built up into a wartime organization of substantial size for that day; but it seems very small indeed when compared with the War Production Board in the recent war.

The War Industries Board had functional divisions set up to deal with such matters as requirements, priorities, price fixing, and so on. Other important divisions were concerned with raw materials and finished products.   The main attention of the Board was given to such urgent matters as the conversion and expansion of industrial facilities, the opening up of new sources of critical raw materials, and the development and operation of a priorities system for the distribution of scarce materials.   Much attention also was given to the conservation of scarce materials, labor, and price control.

The War Industries Board was simply the most important of a score of war agencies set up to deal with problems of production, distribution, and control in a variety of fields.   There was a Fuel Administration, and a Food Administration, a Railroad Administration, and a Shipping Board; and still others dealt with labor, foreign trade, and communications.   Through the priorities power delegated to it by the President, the War Industries Board was able to accomplish a much needed coordination of the economic war effort.

In this mobilization the United States moved very slowly.   Nearly a year passed after the declaration of war before our industrial mobilization began to make real headway.   Not until 13 months after we entered the war was the War Industries Board given the priority power essential for its effective operation.   There was a strong public resistance to the wartime controls.   For example the automobile industry succeeded in opposing all the efforts of the War Industries Board to restrict automobile production until the spring of 1918, a year after we had entered the war.   Then agreement was reached to reduce production to 30 percent of capacity and to end production at the close of 1918, by which time the war was over.   One of the largest of the automobile manufacturers, in fact, refused to go along with the industry in this matter until he was finally brought around by the threat of commandeering his coal supply and denying him the use of any railroad cars.

The mobilization of our economy was nevertheless in many respects a very great achievement.   With only a small head start from Allied orders, we built up a war production system of tremendous capacity. We supplied our Allies with great quantities of food, raw materials, and manufactured articles.   We recruited, trained, equipped, and transported to France an army of over two million men.   We moved from an economy without controls to one which in many respects was highly regimented.

But against this array of achievements must be balanced serious shortcomings.   The early failure to establish central direction and controls in war procurement and production resulted in great delays and in great losses in manpower and materials.   Another serious weakness was failure to sharply restrict nonessential production in order to force industrial conversion to war production.   The mistakes and delays in determination of military requirements and the setting of production goals too high at the beginning resulted in a disproportionate share of labor and materials being absorbed simply in tooling up for production.   As a result of the delays, war production was just getting into high gear when the war came to an end.   Major items of materiel—airplanes, shell cases, and artillery—were supplied to the American Expeditionary Force chiefly by our Allies.   And, finally, the Federal Government gave literally almost no thought to plans for industrial demobilization and reconversion.   The result was that the war ended in as much confusion as it began.

World War I marked our first national experience in the mobilization of the economic system of the nation to meet the tremendous supply requirements of modern war.   When World War II came, although this experience was not always utilized to the fullest advantage, nevertheless the American people and their leaders had a far greater understanding than in 1917 of the enormous burden which modern war imposes on all the productive resources of the nation.

A far clearer conception had been obtained of the many problems of organization, management, and controls which a full mobilization of the economy demands.

MID-TWENTIETH CENTURY

These examples of the problems of providing economic support of warfare at earlier stages in our history are useful in clarifying the nature of economic mobilization in our own time. Basically, the purposes are much the same today as they were more than a century ago. The objective of economic mobilization, now as then, is the maximum support of military operations—support in manpower, in munitions, and in all the material and supplies essential for the equipment and maintenance of armed forces.

Today as in 1776, the amount of support which can be given depends upon the amount of "fat" in the economy that can be diverted from civilian to military uses; that is, upon the surplus beyond the bare requirements of the civilian population and war supporting industries and services which can be used to raise and support the Army, Navy, and Air Force. Today as in 1776 the amount of such support depends, also, upon the ability of the government to capture this surplus for the prosecution of the war.

The differences between economic support of warfare today and in these earlier wars are, however, greater than the similarities. For example, the problems of financing the abnormal expenditures of wartime present far less difficulty today than in either 1776 or 1861, despite the vastly larger sums, proportionately, that have to be raised. This is partly due to the greater wealth and income within the nation which is available for "capture" through taxation or the sale of war bonds. It is due partly, also, to a broader understanding of the problems and possibilities of public finance, and partly to the greater capabilities of the fiscal machinery of the government and the financial institutions of the nation.

On the other hand, the Government can no longer be content simply to capture the surplus of goods produced by the economic system, an objective which would have been more than adequate to the needs of the American Revolution or the Civil War. It is essential in the age of "total war" that all means be employed to increase this surplus by raising the productive capacity and output of the nation to levels that would scarcely be regarded as attainable in peacetime. Moreover, the size, complexity, and exacting requirements of the material of modern war present very difficult problems of converting industrial facilities, equipment, and labor to their production. Warfare has passed far beyond the simple "food-and-forage," "powder-and-shot" stage of our early history.

Some of the differences in warfare as conducted by past generations and in our own time are readily seen and understood—for example, the different weapons employed and the manner in which they are used. In the absence of statistical data it is not easy to grasp the differences in the scale on which different wars in different periods have been waged. Table 1, *"The Rising Cost of Waging War,"* presents a number of major trends relative to the cost of warfare and the means of meeting this cost at different times in our national history. Three basic trends are shown in this table, dealing with population, with national wealth, and with the cost of war, respectively. The population figures are self-explanatory. They display what has been an extraordinary rate of population increase over a period of 175 years: an eightfold increase between the Revolution and the Civil War, a threefold increase between the Civil War and World War I, and another thirty percent rise between World War I and World War II. There has clearly been a tremendous broadening of the manpower base of the economy—the base from which must be drawn the men and women for the Armed Forces and to man the munitions factories and other war supporting industries and services in an emergency.

The statistics of national wealth are no less interesting. By national wealth is meant simply the total value, measured in dollars, of all the durable property within the nation, regardless of whom it belongs to, whether private individuals, business or other organizations, or governments—local, State, and National. It consists mainly of such items as the land and of all buildings and structures upon the land, such equipment as machinery within factories and other buildings and railroads, ships, bridges, roads, and the like. It also includes all inventories of goods. Table 1 shows an increase in this national wealth from three-fourths of a billion dollars to 750 billions. But these figures are not to be taken too literally for two reasons. First, they are estimates and those for the earlier dates are very rough estimates, indeed, with a margin of error which may be wide; and secondly, allowances must be made for marked changes in the value of the dollar in terms of the commodities that the dollar will buy, over this long period of time. As a rough estimate, the dollar of 1775 would probably purchase four times as much commodities—let us say, flour, meat, butter and woolen cloth—as the dollar of the 1940's would buy. In terms of real commodities, then, it will be safer to estimate that the national wealth has increased from 1775 to 1940 *not* one thousand times, but somewhere on the order of two hundred and fifty times.

But while the national wealth has been skyrocketing, so has the population which possesses, in one manner or another, this wealth. We can visualize this trend better, therefore, if we reduce it to per capita terms, thus allowing for the great increase in population.   As the third column indicates, per capita wealth rose nearly twentyfold in terms of dollars; allowance for a fourfold increase in prices gives a fivefold per capita increase of wealth in commodity terms.   The significance of these figures for warfare is readily apparent.   This national wealth, which, in real, commodity terms, has risen five times faster than population, represents facilities, equipment, and goods of all kinds which can either be converted or diverted from the purposes of peace to the prosecution of military operations.   Other things being equal, the greater the national wealth, the larger will be the income derived annually from the utilization of this wealth for productive purposes; and the larger will be the surplus of income which can be channeled into the military budget.   This means that larger armed forces can be raised; and the equipment and supply of these forces can be provided in a manner to secure maximum effectiveness.   One has only to compare the simple muskets, bayonets, swords, and cannon of the Revolutionary armies with the tremendously elaborate, complex, and costly machines of combat in our own time to grasp the significance of the economic changes which have made the new warfare possible.

In the last three columns on the right of table 1 are shown the steady and, in the last seventy-five years, the sharp upward trend in the cost of waging war, considered in terms of total cost of the major wars, of average annual cost for each war, and of per capita annual cost.   Only the direct, monetary costs are shown.   They are round number estimates, but, since data on government expenditures in wartime have been fairly well recorded, these figures are not too far from the mark. Inasmuch as the wars were of varying length, as indicated by the year shown under each war, average annual costs as well as annual per capita costs are shown.

In respect to World War II the question may be raised: With a national wealth of 750 billion dollars, how was the United States able to spend a total of 350 billions in the prosecution of the war without seriously reducing the amount of this national wealth.   It is important to note that these 350 billion dollars were spent over a five-year period, or an average annual expenditure, as noted in the column to the right, of 70 billions.   While the expenditures of the Federal Government were rising to enormous totals during the war years, national income was also increasing (although not as much in proportion) from 81 billion dollars in 1940 to 182 billions in 1945.

It is worth noting that the average annual cost of war has risen much more rapidly than has the national or per capita wealth of the nation. However reckoned, the cost of waging war has reached astronomical levels in our time, imposing a load on the nation's economic system which could not possibly have been borne by the smaller and less advanced economy of a hundred years ago.

Table 1.   The Rising Cost of Waging War*

	Size of population	Total national wealth (millions)	Per capita wealth	Total cost of war (millions)	Average annual cost (millions)	Annual per capita cost of war
Revolutionary War (7 years)_____	2, 500, 000	$750	$300	$125	$17	$7
Civil War (North) (4 years)_____	22, 000, 000	11, 000	500	3, 300	825	38
World War I (2 years)_	100, 000, 000	250, 000	2, 500	35, 000	17, 500	175
World War II (5 years)_____	132, 000, 000	750, 000	5, 700	350, 000	70, 000	530

*The figures in the above table have been calculated and estimated from data presented in the Bureau of the Census publication, Historical Statistics of the United States, 1789–1945.

III

ECONOMIC POTENTIAL FOR WAR

RISE AND DEVELOPMENT OF ECONOMIC POTENTIAL CONCEPT

One should know one's enemies, their alliances, their resources, and the nature of their country in order to plan a campaign. One should know what to expect of one's friends, what resources one has and foresee the future effects to determine what one has to fear or hope from political maneuvers.[1]

The above instructions were written by Frederick the Great in 1747 for his generals, and his advice is much more meaningful today than in the eighteenth century. Armies in his time were small. They fought with muzzle-loading weapons, communicated by messengers and signal fires, and transported their equipment by horse. War was the "sport of kings" and was fought to a considerable extent by mercenaries. Except for tax levies made upon him to maintain the national treasure chest, the civilian was not greatly concerned with wars unless they were fought within his immediate vicinity.

With the wars of the French Revolution conscription was introduced and men spoke of a "nation in arms." In the two World Wars, large proportions of the national resources were employed and the broader concept of a "nation at war" was introduced.[2] In World War I the industrialization of war made men conscious of the possibilities of applying huge volumes of material resources in combat. Here for the first time military forces made use of the airplane, radio communications, and great quantities of motor transportation. Massed heavy artillery and automatic weapons devoured vast tonnages of fabricated metal each day in the form of bullets and shells. Marshal Foch stated that mobilization "Takes up all the intellectual and material resources of the country in order to secure a successful issue," and a British author, commenting on statements such as the foregoing, wrote: "There is hardly an industry or a branch of science which does not in some way contribute to war potential." [3]

When the delegates of the triumphant nations met at Paris in 1919 to consolidate their success, the French representatives stressed the

---

[1] *Frederick the Great, Instructions for His Generals* (translated by Brig. Gen. Thomas R. Phillips), Harrisburg, Pa., Military Service Publishing Co., 1944, p. 24. The first four pages of this chapter are based largely on two ICAF publications on *Economic Potential for War*, R139 and R165.

[2] Dupuy, R. Ernest, "Nations at War," chapter 5 in Brown, Hodges, and Roucek, *Contemporary Politics* (New York: John Wiley & Sons, 1939).

[3] Lefebure, Victor, *Scientific Disarmament* (New York: Macmillan, 1931), p. 31.

underlying importance of the changes that had taken place in warfare. They used the concept of "economic potential for war" and pointed out that, while the Germans had been defeated militarily, they still retained much of their civilian economy. The French contended that this civilian economy could be the base for the redevelopment of German power even if Germany's armed forces were limited by treaty.

The discussions over this point continued, and in the disarmament debates that took place in Geneva during the late 1920's and early 1930's, the subject of economic potential for war was frequently mentioned. Much controversy ensued over the question of including economic potential as a consideration in determining armament limitations. It was contended by some countries, led by France, that, in fixing armament limitations for individual countries, those with less potential should be recompensed by permission to maintain higher levels of actual armaments. Italy, Japan, Belgium, Czechoslovakia, Poland, Rumania, and Yugoslavia followed the lead of the French. The United States, Great Britain, and Germany, for obvious reasons, opposed this view. They were supported by Chile, Finland, the Netherlands, Spain, and Sweden. The United States contended that economic potential for war could not be considered in limiting armaments since such potential could not readily be changed into armaments. This country had been in World War I for 19 months before the Armistice of 1918, yet only four cannons produced here during that period had reached the front. No agreement on the incorporation of economic potential was reached, and, in fact, the whole project for armament limitation failed. The significance of economic potential for war, however, had been brought into prominence.

World War II proved more clearly even than World War I that industrial strength is at the base of national power. The weight of equipment and ammunition used on land and sea and in the air was vastly greater than it had been in the previous struggle. The importance of economic potential to national security had been established in World War I. In World War II it was proved by a mass of evidence that was overwhelming.

IMPACT OF ECONOMIC POTENTIAL ON STRATEGY

The rise of the concept of economic potential has been accompanied by a corresponding change in considerations of strategy. "Military strategy," in the traditional sense, is based largely on personnel and materiel of the Armed Forces. It has given way on the higher levels to "national strategy," which must rely for support not only on the strength and equipment of the Armed Forces, but also on such broader factors as the productive capacity of the Nation and public opinion.

Finally a more comprehensive type of strategy has evolved, based on the military capabilities and economic potential of a group of nations. The planning and direction of such collective national action is called "combined strategy."

Military strategy. At one time most military planners were inclined to emphasize the current and short-range aspects of their studies. They were interested in the military capabilities of the enemy to make and sustain an initial strike, and in their own capabilities for countering that operation. Military studies were short-range, limited to months at most—usually to weeks and days. Factors other than military were largely confined to those acting within the division. Logistic considerations usually went no further than the determination of supplies and equipment available in depots and the means of their distribution to and within the division.

Even with the advance of the military student to studies of strategy in relation to field armies and groups of armies, similar restricted boundaries of his consideration existed. True, he did expand his thinking about logistics to terms of theater supplies rather than forward depots, but usually his analyses were based on the assumption that the zone of interior would furnish to the theater the supplies and equipment which were required. He further tacitly assumed that the State Department would take care of necessary international political arrangements. Economic potential played little part in his thinking.

National strategy. When the officer is faced for the first time with studies of national strategy, it is only natural that he is prone to consider as paramount the military aspects of the situation and is further inclined to spend most of his time upon current and short-range capabilities. His experience in the past has convinced him that the economy of his country can furnish all the supporting material which he requires if only someone in authority orders it done. Only when he examines the logistics requirements of global war, does he begin to realize the fallacy of such thinking. In the light of the wars of this century, it becomes clear that the ultimate victors have been those nations which could, in the long run, furnish the most effective material support to the Armed Forces. The necessity for the analysis of comparative economic strengths accordingly remains vital to national strategy whatever may be the most probable determinant of victory.

Combined strategy. Study of economic and social factors leads to a rough estimation of the potential economic power and the economic potential for war of a single nation. In the modern world, however, nations do not act independently. Hostilities are carried on by one group of nations acting together and opposing another group. The study of the power of a single nation is therefore in itself of limited value until that study has been combined with similar studies of other nations in such a manner that the potential power of the group may be determined. The power of a group is not a summation of the powers of the individual nations, but rather an integration of those powers. Some of the surplus capabilities of each nation are absorbed within the group whereas other capabilities are intensified. The grouping may cause a nation having a normal agricultural surplus to maintain in time of war its total agricultural production in order to furnish food for less self-sufficient nations of the group. On the other hand, some nations may be able to furnish critical raw materials to other industrial nations increasing the latter's capabilities for production of munitions.

Groups of nations working together do experience difficulties which a nation acting independently escapes. The single nation does not meet with the delays and arguments which are a part of the process of reaching a group decision. It does not experience the paralysis that results from the conflict of customs and interests of different countries. In any group of nations, regardless of the intentions of all the member governments to cooperate and work for a common end, there are inherent oppositions, both in the economic and the political fields. To be successful, the group must, therefore, work through a series of compromises which normally result in weaker action than would otherwise be possible.

FACTORS CONSTITUTING ECONOMIC POTENTIAL

Probably no two students would agree in detail on the essential components of the economic strength of a country. The seven factors considered in the following pages, however, are representative of those generally considered in a discussion of the subject, and they are broad enough to include the great majority of the elements that go to make up economic potential. They are: human elements, natural resources, industrial strength, transportation and communication, international trade, the structure of the economy, and economic growth.

1. HUMAN ELEMENTS

a. *The size of the population.* Large numbers of people are required for strength, but numbers alone are not sufficient. If the total sum of human beings were the sole consideration, China would be the most powerful nation in the world; India would follow, and the Soviet Union would come third. As we know, however, the quantity of population, while very important, is frequently secondary to qualitative considerations, such as the cultural endowment and national characteristics of the people.

b. *State of culture.* The term "culture," as used here, refers to the state of advancement in civilization. It is generally believed by anthropologists that most races are approximately equal in native ability. The fact that one appears superior and another inferior is attributed to the difference in cultural development. Thus, the Angles, Saxons, and other Teutonic peoples at the beginning of the Christian era were much lower in the scale of civilization than some others, such as the Greeks and Romans. Nineteen centuries later their descendants, located in other settings and intermingled with similar peoples, were at the top. Their progression is not be explained by improvements in the stock but by their cultural development. The state of culture is determined by such matters as education, the development of industry, science, social habits, and the ability to cooperate in large-scale projects. In 1492 there were about a million American Indians living in what is now continental United States. The country was then invaded by Europeans of a much more advanced culture who were able to make far more efficient use of the natural resources of the New World. This proficiency increased until today there are some 170 million occupying this territory and living according to far higher standards than did the Indians. Under their advanced methods the land yields a thousand fold greater product than in 1492. Their coordinated economic and political projects are vastly greater than anything of which the Indians could have dreamed.

One of the most important aspects of an advanced culture is the capability of a people to protect their health through medical science and sanitary regulations and facilities. When such efforts are effectively made, the death rate is reduced and the average age of the population is increased. It is sometimes thought that a young nation, one which has a large percentage of the population in the younger age groups, is virile and energetic and highly competent for the conduct of industry or war. This is not necessarily so. More often the nations with the higher proportions in the young-age groups are the unhealthful peoples whose high death rates prevent the accumulation of large numbers of older men and women. The typical Asiatic nation, with some 70 percent of its population under 35, is less productive and less capable of waging modern mechanized war than is the United States which has less than 60 percent under that age. One should not, however, overlook the future potentialities of large backward populations. As they adopt the techniques of western civilization, their proficiency will increase. And when countries like China acquire much better sanitary and medical knowledge, the drop in the death rate can be expected to generate population pressures that may well prove to be among the most explosive forces in international politics.

c. *Occupational distribution of the population.* The distribution of employment by types of industries is a reflection of the structure of the economy and an indication of the extent to which both manpower and production can be diverted to war purposes. A high percentage of the population tied to the land by the necessity of producing food for the remainder of the people, for example, limits the size of the industrial labor force and of the armed forces which may be created in time of war.

d. *Nationalism.* One of the most powerful political influences in the world today is the psychological force that binds together a culturally similar people, occupying a common area, into a united community—the nation. The nation aspires to, and in most cases has achieved, its own government in the nation-state. It strongly resists efforts of a foreign imperialistic power to impose controls upon it and even is inclined to reject, sometimes in an uncooperative manner, any efforts by an international organization that are regarded as infringing upon its sovereignty. The cultural ties that bind fellow nationals together are those of common language, religion, customs, historic experiences, and ideology, although no one of these is absolutely essential. The advantage in economic potential of a nationalistic people over one that is not, lies in the willingness of its citizens to join in the common projects of the nation, even though they may require personal sacrifices. Without a strong sense of nationalism among its citizens a government cannot carry out large projects, either military or economic, that require important unselfish contributions on the part of large numbers of people.

2. NATURAL RESOURCES

a. *Physical geography.* The size of the land is today a matter of great importance. Shortly after the break-up of feudalism, some small and moderately sized countries, because of their industry and commercial initiative, gained much success in commerce, war, and empire building. Beginning in the 15th century, Portugal and Spain, and later Holland, France, and Great Britain, occupying altogether only a small area on the globe, spread their power outward until at one time or another these countries controlled a large part of the earth's surface. They operated with the cheapest and quickest means of transportation, the sailing vessel. The coming of better land transportation, starting in the 19th century, made it possible to organize effectively the large interior land masses. Since then the size of the most effective land units has grown until today the strongest economic-military units, the United States (3 million square miles) and the USSR (8 million square miles), seem almost continental in size. Population, food supply, resources, and large industrial systems, bound together by interior lines of transportation and communication, give these land masses certain superiorities as compared with smaller countries.

Despite the advantage of the large land mass a favorable position of a nation with respect to routes of ocean communication is of much importance since it provides a means for maintaining commerce with other parts of the world and thus increasing its economic potential. The desire of a land-locked nation for deep-water ports is motivated by the hope of adding to its economic potential the advantage of direct trade with the sources of goods and materials that lie overseas.

The climate may have much to do with the strength and well-being of the population. It appears to be no accident that the great world powers have all been located in the temperate zones where the climate is moderate. Through history man has seemed to be at his best, both mentally and physically, within this zone. Climatic conditions also affect directly the share of national production which must be expended on clothing and shelter.

b. *Agricultural resources.* The size and topography of the land, the chemical and physical characteristics of the soil, the humidity, and the length of the growing season determine the extent to which a nation may be self-sufficient in the production of food and agricultural materials essential to industry. Together with these influences must be considered the state of agricultural science and technology.

c. *Mineral resources.* The extent to which a nation is self-sufficient within its own borders affects its potential power. No industrial nation is fully self-sufficient. Its supply must be composed not only of minerals that are domestically produced but also of those that are imported. While imported minerals are often essential, it is important to be able to produce internally as much of the supply as possible. Thus the iron and steel industry could hardly exist in a country which produced neither iron nor coal. That industry is normally located at a place near or of easy access to one or both of these minerals. An additional reason for desiring domestic production of essential minerals is the risk in time of war of loss of imported supply through blockade or other action of the enemy.

Not only is the possession of a mineral supply important but the relative locations of different minerals within a country have a bearing on the economic development and resulting potential strength of that country. The tremendous distances between many of the iron ore bodies and the coal mines of Russia have made difficult the development of the Soviet steel industry. The United States, on the other hand, has been particularly fortunate in that its ore deposits and its coal mines are connected by routes of easy transportation, consisting of navigable rivers and the Great Lakes, a water system that is supplemented by good railways. Along these routes of transportation have also existed the areas favorable for the growth of centers of population and industry. Minerals, transportation, and labor have been combined to build the steel industry in the Pittsburgh, Youngstown, and Chicago areas. In Birmingham, even more happily, the ore bodies and coal mines are in close proximity to each other. The supplementary value to the steel industry of foreign minerals is shown by the importation of manganese and, in some cases, iron ore. More than ninety percent of the manganese used in the American steel industry is imported, the chief sources being Africa, India, Brazil, and Cuba. With the decline of iron ore supplies in the United States the amount imported has been increasing. One steel mill at Sparrows Point near Baltimore imports ore from South America and Sweden, while it obtains its coal from Pennsylvania and West Virginia.

Reserves of minerals are a great economic asset, but other things are required to make these resources usable. Mining technology and facilities and, as has been pointed out, a transportation system are of great importance in determining mineral production. Minerals without the means of extracting them are of little real value. Accordingly the figures for annual production by countries of the principal essential minerals present a better picture of mineral strength for the near future than does a tabulation of estimated reserves.

In estimating the economic and military strength of a country, some analysts place great emphasis on coal and iron production. One of the country's leading mineralogists calls attention to the fact that previous to World War II the countries that were to be the leading belligerents were also the leading coal-producing nations. The fact that in this contest the victory went to the side of greater coal production should not, he said, be regarded as mere coincidence.[4]

A specific case of comparing mineral output will help to illustrate the nature of this type of evaluation of economic potential. Figures for coal and iron ore production are herewith given for four selected countries in the Orient and the West: India, Japan, the United Kingdom, and the United States.

Table 2.   Coal and Iron Ore Production, 1952*

[Thousands of metric tons]

	Coal	Iron ore
India	36, 885	2, 550
Japan	43, 359	737
United Kingdom	230, 125	4, 948
United States	457, 590	50, 013

*United Nations, *Statistical Yearbook*, 1954. Tables 38 and 43. This is the most useful published source of information regarding the economies of the various countries.

4 Pehrson, Elmer Walter, "Problems of United States Mineral Supply," *Annals of the American Academy of Political and Social Science*, November, 1951, p. 167.

3. INDUSTRIAL STRENGTH

In seeking to compare the economic potential of various nations, no single factor is more important than industrial strength. The ability of a people to transform raw materials into commodities like steel or aluminum and to manufacture items like tractors, airplanes, and other machines is essential in the conduct of mechanized warfare. Out of the mills and factories come the tremendous volumes of guns, ammunition, and equipment necessary in modern combat. There is no single index that can measure accurately the industrial strength of a country. Yet each one can contribute something to a general estimate. A few of the indexes, including those for steel output, energy production, and gross national product, will be discussed in the following pages.

a. *The annual steel output.* The steel industry is frequently regarded as a good indicator of the industrialization of the country. The figures for steel manufacture reflect the demands made by a wide range of other industries, for production equipment, capital installations, and durable consumer goods. Thus, when the production of steel in any country rises, it is a rough indication of the growth of industrial activity generally.

b. *Energy production.* The production of energy would be a valuable indicator of national strength if it could be accurately measured. The total production of power bears a fairly close relationship to total industrial production. Energy, however, comes from many sources and for some of these there are no statistical data. In the case of electrical energy, figures of kilowatt hour consumption are reported. These, however, give a greater emphasis to those countries with the most modern systems of production, perhaps greater emphasis than their productivity warrants. Following are figures for steel and energy reported by selected countries for the year 1952.

Table 3.   Steel and Electrical Production, 1952*

	Crude steel production (thousands of metric tons)	Electrical energy production (millions of KWH)	Energy consumption per person (in terms of tons of coal)
India	1, 603	6, 120	0. 11
Japan	6, 988	51, 647	0. 9
United Kingdom	16, 681	63, 897	4. 6
United States	84, 520	463, 055	7. 8

*United Nations, *Statistical Yearbook, 1954*, Tables 110, 123, and 125.

It will be seen that the relative ranking of the countries is the same in both columns but that the United States has a considerably greater leadership in electrical energy than in steel.

c. *Gross national product and national income.* A comprehensive index, if it could be computed and compared accurately, would be either the gross national product (GNP) or the national income (NI). The gross national product is the total product of goods and services within the nation expressed in monetary terms.   The national income is a somewhat reduced figure, obtained by subtracting from the GNP the amount of depreciation of durable capital goods and the sum representing indirect business taxes.   While both the GNP and the NI include many things beside industrial output, nevertheless they rise and fall with the state of industry and bear an approximate relationship to industrial strength.   There are two obstacles to the use of the GNP and NI.   In the first place the methods of arriving at these figures are not standardized throughout the world, and they accordingly give results that are not always strictly comparable.   In the second place, since they are expressed in the currency of the particular country there should be some precise method of converting them into a common unit of value.   Yet currencies in the present upset state of the world, with various degrees of inflation and with numerous financial black markets set up because of the inaccuracy of official exchange rates, are difficult to compare.

Table 4.   Estimate of National Income, 1950*

[Billions of dollars]

India	20
Japan	9
United Kingdom	32
United States	240

*United Nations, *Statistical Yearbook, 1954.* Foreign currencies are translated into dollars through use of exchange rates given in Table 158.

The GNP and the NI are, however, of considerable value, not only in determining the overall productivity of a country but also in analyzing the economic structure of that country.   They show with a fair degree of accuracy what percentages are derived from the major classes of economic activity.

There are several reasons for caution in using production figures in comparing economic potential.   Production rises and falls with business activity, and in times of depression it will be considerably below plant capacity.   In such a case the statistics of output would not be an accurate index of economic potential.   Another reservation to be made is that overall production figures do not indicate how closely industry is relative to war uses or how easily convertible to military purposes.   A powerful peacetime economy which is incapable of rapid conversion to the production of war goods will not be as immediately effective in time of war as a weaker economy that can begin the production of munitions immediately or without great delay.   Heavy industries make more contribution to a war effort with less need of radical change than light, consumer-goods industries.

In this respect certain policies of the U. S. S. R. for building up economic potential for war should be noted.   The Soviet regime was born during war.   The U. S. S. R. has since stabilized itself from time to time by stressing the threat of foreign foes.   The peacetime preparation of industry for war has been a feature of the various 5-year plans, which have placed emphasis upon heavy industry, including the production of munitions, while the consumer-goods industries have been severely limited.   The annual production of steel in Russia has risen from 4 million tons in 1928 to 45 million in 1954 or to approximately half the American production.   Much of Russian steel goes to support military plans.   It is possible that the Soviet Union has available for military purposes more steel than has the United States despite the greater American production figures.

4. TRANSPORTATION AND COMMUNICATION

The proportion of human, natural, and industrial resources that a nation will be able to draw upon in a war effort depends in large measure upon the transportation and communication systems within the country.   These are the arterial and nervous systems that make it possible for a national economy to function.   The ability to connect raw material supplies, manufacturing plants, and markets in a cheap and rapid system of transportation is of the utmost importance in the development of large-scale industry.   It was the improvement of land transportation that made it possible for countries of large interior land masses to become effective economic and military units.   Rapid communication is important in the conduct of business on a national scale and also in developing a sense of national unity.   During World War II the thousands of long-distance telephone conversations held between government officials and military officers in Washington and business men, officials, and officers throughout the country helped to make possible a centrally controlled system of war production.   Transportation and communication have made possible the diffusion of intelligence and national sentiments in this country from coast to coast.   At one time it was frequently asserted that a land area as large as the United States today could not be united under a democratic form of government.   The sectional interests within such a country would be too diverse, and the people of one region would have little knowledge of events in another.   Today with instantaneous communication by telegraph, telephone, radio, and television, the chief events of one area can be known in the most remote American communities sooner than they would have been reported in earlier days a few miles from the point of their occurrence.

Transportation and communication are parts of the industrial and social system, holding a relationship of both cause and effect. They contribute to and result from the strength of the economy. Their statistics furnish another index by which national economic strength can be estimated and by which it can be compared with that of another country. Figures regarding transportation and communication include facilities (lines and equipment) and usage (car loadings, ton miles, and messages sent). It would be dangerous to place too much emphasis on any one characteristic of transportation and communication, such as pipeline or railway mileage or number of television sets. Large land countries may show considerable railway mileage while seaboard countries will naturally have more ships than those whose activity is in the interior. Each characteristic will have importance in the total picture, but cannot be relied upon standing by itself.

Table 5. Some Figures Regarding Transportation and Communication for Selected Countries, 1952*

	Railways, passenger— kilometers (millions)	Railways, tons— kilometers (millions)	Automobiles, passenger cars in use (thousands)	Automobiles, commercial vehicles (thousands)	Merchant shipping tons (thousands)	No. of domestic telegrams sent and received (thousands)	No. of telephones in use (thousands)
India_____	57, 994	47, 356	160	121	477	23, 785	179
Japan_____	81, 282	38, 724	59	195	2, 787	91, 494	2, 240
United Kingdom_____	33, 297	36, 613	2, 561	1, 037	18, 624	36, 400	5, 927
United States_____	54, 771	902, 180	43, 654	8, 962	27, 245	151, 710	48, 056

*United Nations, *Statistical Yearbook, 1954.*

The foregoing table reinforces the point just made; i. e., that no one of these statistics by itself can be conclusive or even to an important extent indicative of total economic potential. It must be taken into consideration in connection with other statistics showing the conditions peculiar to the particular country. Thus the fact that Americans aparently make less use of railway passenger service than do the people of India and Japan must be considered in connection with the vastly greater use in the United States of busses and private automobiles. The low figures for railway freight movement in Japan and the United Kingdom must be weighed in relation to the large proportionate use of coastwise shipping by those countries.

5. INTERNATIONAL TRADE

a. *The nature of international trade.* The ability of a country to import goods and materials to supply deficiencies in its domestic production helps to build up its economic potential. International trade is conducted during peacetime on the principle that a particular country may benefit by exchanging commodities which it can produce with relative ease and cheapness for those which it needs but which it can produce, if at all, only at relatively high cost. Thus the United States, which is unable to raise bananas cheaply, imports them from such countries as Honduras where bananas can be grown at low cost. In return this country sends manufactured items, such as mining machinery, which Honduras cannot well produce. Great Britain has for generations exported manufactured goods and imported raw materials. Saudi Arabia exports oil and in return imports machinery and other products of the West. Imports are an addition to the wealth of a country, and, in most cases, they augment its economic potential. Exports are a subtraction from wealth in the case of commodities which are often easily produced domestically. Their exchange for commodities which are relatively hard to produce constitutes a net gain to the country's economy.

b. *What trade figures show regarding economic potential.* A large foreign trade indicates an active economy, one which profits from the system of international specialization and exchange. Exports tend to show industrial superiority and the ability to sell manufactured goods in the world market or they may mean cheap land and richness of resources that make it possible to produce low-cost crops and raw materials. Imports denote an ability to enrich the economy by procurement from abroad. They may also spot-light weaknesses in domestic production—the lack of a vital element. The United States needs manganese for steel manufacture; the people of the United Kingdom cannot live without importing food. Whether these needs would be serious weaknesses in time of war depends upon the location of the source of supply, the hazards of the trade routes, and, in case of industrial materials, the possibility of substitutes as well as the size of the stockpile.

6. STRUCTURE OF THE ECONOMY

When the national product is divided according to its origin into the various segments of economic activity, a rough picture of the nature of the economy can be obtained. The percentages that come from agriculture, manufacturing, trade, etc., can be determined, and a great deal of light can be thrown upon the economic potential of the country for war. A country with a low standard of living and one in which a large percentage of the national product is derived from agriculture has comparatively few excess resources to devote to war. Since the population is close to a subsistence level, men cannot easily be diverted from work in the fields. On the other hand a country with a high standard of living with a large proportion of the population engaged in manufacture can convert a considerable proportion of its facilities and energies to war. Many manufactured products can be dispensed with in an austerity program during war and the manufacturing plants turned to war production. Thus the American automobile industry was converted to the manufacture of planes, tanks, and other munitions during World War II. The United States, without any really important civilian loss, had turned to war purposes a tremendous industrial force.

The following table shows the breakdown of the "net geographical product" of the four countries that were previously considered. The net geographical product is similar to the national income except that it excludes income received from and includes income paid to the rest of the world.

Table 6.   Economic Structure of Selected Countries Net Geographical Product by Industrial Origin, 1950.*

	Total (billions)	Agriculture, forestry, fishing, mining (Percent of total)	Manufacturing, construction (Percent of total)	Trade, transport, communications (Percent of total)	Public administration, defense (Percent of total)	Other (Percent of total)
India	$20	52	15	17	5	11
Japan	10	25	30	26	4	15
United Kingdom	33	9	43	24	6	18
United States	240	9	36	27	10	18

*Based on UN, Statistical Yearbook, 1954, table 157.

7. ECONOMIC GROWTH

The factors previously considered deal mainly with existing economic conditions. It becomes important, however, to consider also the trend of development of the national economies. The knowledge of trends will help us to determine, as far as possible, what the relative economic power of nations will be in the years to come. The comparative strength of states is continuously changing in the international kaleidoscope. The number one country of one generation may be second or third in the next. It is desirable, therefore, to investigate the speed of economic growth and the particular fields in which such growth is taking place.

a. *Free enterprise and the growth of the United States.* One of the outstanding economic phenomena of the later 19th and earlier 20th centuries was the spectacular industrial rise of the United States. With rich resources at their command and with freedom from many of the social and political hindrances existing in Europe, Americans threw themselves enthusiastically into the task of economic development. The motivation sprang from individual opportunity, the opportunity of the individual to improve his own status and to rise, in many cases, in one generation from rags to riches. In times of peace there was very little thought given to the development of the American economy for purposes of national security. Under the impulse of the ambition of the individual for himself and his family, however, seeming miracles were performed. In 1879 the production of steel ingots and castings in this country was 935,273 tons. A half century later, in 1929, the output was 56,433,473 tons. Through a formula to be explained later, the average annual growth of steel production over this period was at the very high rate of 8.5 percent. This is only one indication of the expansion of American industry during a half century that saw the United States rising to undisputed industrial preeminence. During this period the United States became a great world power.

b. *The planned growth of the Soviet Union.* The Soviet Union, with its various 5-year plans, has given far greater attention to the planning of economic growth than have the countries of the West where free enterprise prevails. The USSR has thrown much energy into a nationally designed effort to make itself the most powerful country in the world. The development of the Soviet economy, if the motivation were to be derived from communist theory, would no doubt have as its main objective the improvement of the standard of living of the proletariat. That objective, however, has been displaced as the leading Soviet purpose by the desire to increase the country's economic potential for war. Light industries for producing consumer goods have taken second place to heavy industries and munitions making. Steel production, so important in war, for example, has been emphasized in the various plans, and, as we shall see, has greatly increased. Prior to World War I the Ukraine was almost the only steel-producing area in the USSR. In the intervening years expansion has taken place, not only in the Ukraine, but also in many places in the Urals and Central Siberia. The rate of growth in Soviet steel production has been much greater during this time than in the important steel-producing areas of the Free World. However, the Soviet rate has been equaled and even exceeded in some western countries which have had almost no steel industry and where the percentages of growth caused by only moderate new developments have accordingly been high.

c. *Some elementary comparisons.* A specialist in the economy of any particular foreign country may be able, through years of research, to piece together an estimate of the overall economic growth of that country from information obtained through its economic literature. Principles of evaluating that literature must be developed. No such thorough effort can be made here. Rather, some very simple comparisons will be drawn with the understanding, of course, that such comparisons have definite limitations. Only easily available figures will be used, and the purpose will be merely to introduce the subject of measuring rates of economic development.

d. *The formula for the rate of growth.* Economic growth is conveniently summarized in the annual rate of increase; that is, the percentage by which the production of each year has, on the average over a period, exceeded that of the previous year. When the economic status of a country or of an aspect of its economy is represented by a figure in a given year and by a larger figure several years later, the annual rate of increase is obtained by a formula similar to that for computing the rate of compound interest necessary to produce a given principal in a given time. Let F equal the first figure in the series; L, the last figure; N, the number of years considered; and R, the rate of increase. The formula is as follows:

$$\frac{L}{F} = (1+R)^N$$

Given the steel production of the Soviet Union for 1928 at 4,251,000 metric tons and that for 1953 at 38,000,000, the substitutions in the formula are:

$$\frac{38,000,000}{4,251,000} = (1+R)^{25}$$

or $\qquad\qquad 8.94 = (1+R)^{25}$

Taking the 25th root of both sides of the equation, we have:

$$1.092 = 1 + R$$
$$R = .092$$

Thus, during the years under consideration, Soviet steel production increased at the very high rate of 9.2 percent per year.

e. *Comparison of rates of growth in steel production.* Steel is a basic commodity in munitions and also in the expansion of other industries, both in war and peace. The increase in steel production is therefore an important factor in the growth of economic potential for war. Steel is also a convenient commodity to use because figures of steel production are more easily ascertained for countries behind the iron curtain than are the statistics for many other activities. The following table shows the increases in production from 1928 to 1953.

Table 7.   Crude Steel Production, 1928–53*

[Thousands of metric tons]

	1928	1953	Annual rate of increase
Brazil---	21	1, 002	. 167
Canada-----------------------------------	1, 255	3, 734	. 045
India----------------------------------	416	1, 531	. 053
Japan---------------------------------	1, 906	7, 662	. 057
Poland--------------------------------	1, 438	3, 604	. 037
USSR----------------------------------	4, 251	38, 000	. 092
United Kingdom-----------------------	8, 656	17, 891	. 029
United States-------------------------	52, 371	101, 250	. 027

*Columns for 1928 and 1953 obtained from United Nations, *Statistical Yearbook, 1948,* Table 104, and *Statistical Yearbook, 1954,* Table 233. For high rates of recent increase in steel production, starting from a small base, in Communist China and also Formosa, see United Nations, *Economic Bulletin for Asia and the Far East,* Vol. VI, No. 2, August 1955, p. 15.

This table indicates a considerably slower rate of growth for the United States than for Russia in steel production. It has been pointed out, however, that the United States, whose steel production expanded rapidly from 1880 to World War I has slowed down in its rate of growth and that the Russian speed of expansion is now similar to that of the United States during this earlier period. If Russia follows the line of American experience, its rate of growth in steel production will likewise slow down as the annual supply becomes more nearly sufficient for its needs. A report prepared for the Joint Committee on the Economic Report has the following to say on the subject:

There is, in fact, a remarkable similarity between the tonnage growth of steel output in the Soviet Union since 1920 and the rate of growth of steel production in the United States and Western Europe between 1880 and 1913. If the Soviet Union should succeed in producing 60 million tons in 1960 its production will be greater that that attained in the United States in 1920 and the 40-year lag will be narrowed. If, on the other hand, Soviet steel production follows the line of what appears to be the longtime trend its production will be about equal to production in the United States in 1920.[5]

There is serious reason to doubt, however, that the Russian curve of steel production will conform to that of the United States over the preceding 40 years. The motivation that produces steel in the Soviet Union is radically different from that which affected earlier American steel production. In the United States, the steel industry from 1880 to 1913 operated to supply private industry. It expanded during prosperity and contracted during depression. Soviet industry is governmentally planned, largely for a purpose beyond the satisfaction of peacetime industrial needs. In fact, the needs of industry are frequently pushed into the background by the demands of national power. It seems very unlikley, therefore, that the rate of growth of its steel industry will conform to the curve established by the United States. It seems also unlikely that it can continue at its present pace of expansion. It ought to be pointed out, however, that if Soviet steel produtcion should continue to grow at a rate of 9.2 percent per year and that of the United States at a rate of 2.7 percent, the Russian output would about equal that of the United States by the year 1969.

Since steel production in the Soviet Union has been much emphasized in the 5-year plans, its rate of growth is above that for Russian industry as a whole. The rate of general economic growth of the Soviet Union during the last 5 years has been placed at between 5 and 6 percent as compared with between 2 and 3 percent for the Free World as a whole. The rate of economic growth of the United States over a similar period, as derived from the figures of the gross national product (1948–53), is slightly under 5 percent. In some particular respects the American rate of growth goes far beyond that of any other country in the world. Thus, that for television-set production over the 5 years mentioned has been about 50 percent per year. In the basic steel industry so important in war, however, as has been shown, American production growth is much below that of Russia. While the quantity of American output is now much higher than that of the Soviet Union, we are apparently faced with serious future rivalry from Russia in the field of economic potential for war.

f. *Some causes of economic growth: the ambition of a nation.* The chief influence behind economic growth is the ambition of a nation, expressed either through unorganized individuals or the Government, to improve its system of production. In a static community no such ambition exists. People are satisfied with the ways of their ancestors. If under those circumstances someone proposes measures to bring about a substantial improvement, he is confronted with apathy

[5] *Trends in Economic Growth,* 83d Cong., 2d Sess., Joint Committee Print, 1955, p. 34.

and regarded with suspicion. He is considered irreverent toward ancient fetishes and an evil influence in general. When, however, there arises among a people a burning desire for progress, psychological obstacles can be more easily overcome and programs leading to economic development are eagerly supported. The spirit of economic progress may be induced by a developing desire of individuals to improve their station in life. Or it may come out of a political motive, as in Russia, to build a socialist state with great strength for war. Even in the United States some of our more recent economic progress must be attributed to the desire for national security and governmentally directed industrial expansion for that purpose.

The zeal for industrial progress can hardly be effective unless accompanied by a considerable degree of national unity. Serious internal controversies, insurrections, or civil war will hold back economic development. Also such development requires the existence of natural resources or the ability to procure them from abroad.

After a national desire for economic progress has been built up, certain intermediate steps are necessary before the rate of economic growth can increase to any considerable extent. The chief steps are an improvement in technology and an investment of capital in production facilities.

Technological improvement. The ambition for improvement results in a rising technology, and the effect of technological development on the rate of production can be illustrated in all fields of industry. The invention and perfection of power-driven machinery was a necessary part of the industrial revolution, as it has been a part of the great economic development of the western nations since that time. The peoples of the West, making use of mechanized methods, have staged over a period of not quite two centuries the most sensational industrial and commercial expansion in history. One illustration taken from the American sulfur industry will be used to make more specific the effect of technology upon production. At the beginning of the 20th century the production of sulfur in this country was small, and most of the American supply was imported, largely from Italy. Sulfur had been exceedingly difficult to mine through several hundred feet of quicksand and sea mud that overlay some of the richest deposits. In 1903 the Frasch process of extracting sulfur was adopted for use. Dr. Frasch, an American chemist, after a dozen years of experimentation, had perfected a method of melting the sulfur in the earth with super-heated steam and then pumping it to the surface. Thus it became relatively easy to extract this mineral. In 1903 the production of sulfur in this country was 35,098 tons. Production during the next half century has risen above 5 million tons, or to about 150 times the 1903 production. The increase has been due almost entirely to the

Frasch process. From an importer of sulfur the United States has become the world's greatest exporter, producing about 40 percent of the world supply Thus, because of a technological improvement one of our formerly less successful industries staged a spectacular development.

The great American advantage in technology after World War II lay in the large numbers of our applied scientists, engineers and technicians. The United States far exceeded the USSR in this respect and therefore possessed a great advantage in the race for economic superiority. This country is now, however, steadily losing this advantage. According to an estimate given by Lewis L. Strauss, Chairman of the Atomic Energy Commission in 1955, the Russian production of trained engineers and scientists for the decade 1950–60 will total about 1,200,000 while that of the United States with something like 900,000 will fall far short of this. Mr. Strauss further stated:

> More than half of all Russian university graduates are in the science-mathematics fields; only one-fifth of our graduates are in those fields. Russian Ph. D.'s, or the equivalent, are three to one in favor of science and engineering; in the United States the ratio is just the reverse—nearly three doctorates in the humanities for every one in science and mathematics.[6]

Unless the American indifference toward world rivalry in science and engineering changes drastically, this generation may witness the first stages of the technological eclipse of the United States and the scientific triumph of communism.

Capital investment. There are two chief methods by which capital flows into industry: (1) that of private initiative and (2) that of governmental decision. Under the free enterprise system individual savings find their way into stocks and bonds and thus furnish funds for investment. Corporations also reinvest part of their earnings in the building of capital facilities. The capacity of a people for saving requires that there be a margin of income above the amount necessary for subsistence. The ability of financiers and industrialists to attract funds into investment depends on the hope of expected returns to be derived from the investment. Funds may be procured through governmental action by taxation, borrowing (either voluntary or compulsory), and the reinvestment of the profits of state-owned enterprises.

In the United States the methods of free enterprise have been used for the most part to procure funds for capital expansion. Governmental action has been employed for capital construction in war and

---

[6] "Freedom's Need for the Trained Man," remarks to the Sixth Thomas Alvin Edison Foundation Institute, East Orange, N. J., November 2, 1955.

in times of depression. It has also been used for the construction of certain kinds of peacetime industries, such, for example, as a few large hydro-power projects. The United States has also used governmental methods to acquire funds for foreign aid. Russia has obtained funds for expansion through the various means of governmental action. This at times has been a severe process because of the low standard of living of the Russian people. In comparing the rate of investment of the United States with that of the USSR, one student of the subject comes to the conclusion that the Soviet rate of investment $\left(\dfrac{capital}{net\ investment}\right)$ has been higher than that in the United States. In nonwar and nondepression years, he states, the American rate of net investment has been 6% to 11%, while in the USSR it has been about 12% to 15%.[7] The higher Soviet rate may show the greater need for improving the production base in Russia. It also shows the ability of the Soviet government to attract or to wring funds from the national economy.

A COMPARISON OF THE ECONOMIES OF INDIA AND JAPAN

To illustrate the principles of measuring economic potential, their application in a brief comparison of the economies of India and Japan will be attempted. This comparison is approached with a strong prejudice, based largely on past performance, that Japan is the stronger. Most of the facts will tend to bear out Japanese superiority. On the other hand the evidence is not entirely consistent on this point, and some indexes point to the greater strength of India, particularly in promise for the future. The comparison is based largely on the data of 1952, the latest year for which complete figures can be found in the most recent edition of the United Nations' Statistical Yearbook.

Population. In 1952 the populations of the two countries were: India, 367 million; Japan, 85.5 million. India surpasses Japan by a ratio of more than four to one. The death rate per 1,000 population in India, however, is 13.6; that in Japan is 8.9. The daily food consumption per person is estimated at 1,590 calories for India, 2,210 for Japan. When qualitative factors are considered, Japan has some strong advantages. The literacy rate is believed to be around 90 percent as compared with 20 percent for India. There is language unity in Japan whereas in India there are 14 main languages and more than 200 different variations in dialect. Language unity is one of the most important means of developing national spirit, and goes far to explain the earlier rise of nationalism among the Japanese.

[7] Norman M. Kaplan in Bergson, Abram (editor), *Soviet Economic Growth,* White Plains, N. Y., Row, Peterson and Co., 1953, p. 46.

An important step to set the cultural stage for national unity in India is the adoption of Hindi as the official language, although English is for the time a permissible alternative. There is a vast amount of educational work to be done, however, before Hindi can be used by the entire populace as a native tongue. Another intangible factor that has prevented the rise of nationalism in India has been the bitter religious conflict between the Moslems and Hindus. The discord has been greatly moderated by the creation of Pakistan, which removed from the population of India almost two-thirds of the Moslems. By the elimination of some 50 million Moslems from Indian society, a serious obstacle to national unity that existed in the older India has been notably reduced.

Natural resources. India has the ultimate advantage of a large, although yet undeveloped, land mass, a "sub-continent." Japan, on the other hand, is a series of islands constituting a country of relatively small size. India is 1,222,000 square miles in area as compared with 143,000 for Japan. Japan is weak in iron ore and coking coal reserves. India has some good sources of coking coal and large bodies of iron ore. Coal production in 1952 was 36,885,000 metric tons for India and 43,359,000 for Japan. Iron ore production for these two countries respectively was 2,550,000 and 737,000 metric tons. The prospects for an iron and steel industry, so far as natural resources are concerned, appear brighter in India than Japan. Rice production in India was 34 million metric tons while that for Japan was 12 million. The effect of climate on the energy of the people, according to principles previously stated, gives some advantage to Japan, which is in the temperate zone while India lies largely within the tropics.

Industrial strength. A comparison of industrial strength reveals a wide difference between the countries, Japan being considerably superior in the heavy industries, so valuable in war. It will be recalled from table 3 that the production of steel in 1952 was 1,603,000 metric tons for India and 6,988,000 for Japan. The production of electrical energy was 6 million kwh's for India and 52 million for Japan, excellent testimony of the greater degree of modernization of Japanese industry. Commercial consumption of energy, expressed in terms of coal, was, for each person, .11 metric tons for India and .9 for Japan. Figures of national income show a greater total amount of economic activity on the part of India, due no doubt to the effort necessary to feed, clothe, and house 367 million people, even though the standard of living is lower than in Japan. The Indian national income, translated into dollars at 21 cents per rupee, amounted in 1950 to $20 billion. The Japanese national income, with the yen at .2778 cents, was $9 billion. The per capita income of Japan, on the other hand, was $108 or almost twice that of India's $57.

When the social and industrial strength of the two countries is compared on the basis of the facilities and usage of their transportation systems, a mixed result is obtained. Table 5 shows that the employment of railways is roughly the same in the two countries, although it can be readily estimated that the per capita use in Japan is much greater. There are more passenger automobiles in India and fewer commercial vehicles than in Japan. Japan is considerably ahead in ocean shipping. In domestic communications Japan is also far in the lead. The evidence regarding transportation and communication on the whole leads to the conclusion that Japan has a considerably more modernized and energized society.

International trade. The figures on the foreign trade of India and Japan seem to fit in well with the picture already established. While the total of exports and imports is about the same for the two countries, an analysis of the type of articles bought and sold internationally shows Japan as an industrialized country, importing food and raw materials and exporting manufactured products. India's trade has a much less pronounced tendency in this direction. Japan sells iron and steel products and cotton fabrics. India's principal exports are light commodities, such as jute bags, tea, coir yarn, as well as cotton goods.

*Table 8. Comparison of Foreign Trade of India and Japan in Major Classifications, 1951**

[Millions of dollars]

	Food	Raw materials	Manufactures and semimanufactures	Other	Total
India—imports	538	478	676	114	1, 806
exports	285	347	757	84	1, 473
Japan—imports	485	1, 184	272	------	1, 941
exports	67	41	1, 220	27	1, 355

*Compiled from figures in U. S. Department of Commerce, *Foreign Commerce Yearbook, 1951.*

Altogether the figures show the Japanese to be more active per capita in foreign trade and to be much more proficient in certain industries that are exceedingly important in war.

Economic structure. Referring to table 6, it is to be noted that in India slightly over half of the geographical product is derived from agriculture. More than half that of Japan comes from manufacturing, construction, trade, transport, and communications. These latter segments of the economy usually mean more in terms of national power than does agriculture. It may be noted that the dollar value of the product from manufacturing and construction is the same in India as in Japan. It has already been stated in connection with the discussion of foreign trade, however, that the manufacturing activities in which Japan excels are in the field of steel and machinery while those of India are largely in jute and cotton textile manufacturing.

Economic growth. The efforts made internally and with outside assistance to develop the economies of India and Japan constitute a story in themselves. Such efforts may be expected to succeed in proportion to the ability and willingness of the people, the resources at hand, the amount of capital made available, and freedom from the devastations of revolution and war.

In contrasting the economic growth of the two countries, we find that in the 16 years from 1937 to 1953 industrial production grew in India at the rate of 2.5 percent per year and in Japan at 1.4 percent.[8] The smallness of Japanese increase was due in large part to the losses from industrial conversion and devastation in World War II. At the present time the Japanese are recovering rapidly from these losses, and their production is increasing much faster than that of India. The rates per year from 1948 to 1953 were India, 4.4 percent, and Japan, 20.8 percent. From this mixture of statistical trends it is difficult to compare accurately the present capabilities for economic growth of these two countries. Aside from the production statistics there are reasons that might lead to the belief that the future is more on the side of India than of Japan. The earlier unification and national spirit of Japan and the planned industrialization of that country, beginning in the 19th century, caused the Japanese to experience a precocious transformation from a feudal to a modern power and placed at their disposal a great economic potential for war. They became easily the strongest of the Asiatic nations. The larger population and land resources of India, however, are great ultimate assets. These sleeping resources await the impending social development of the Indian people before conversion into an imminent and powerful potentiality.

In the earlier history of the western world certain small maritime nations were, like Japan, precociously developed. From the 15th to the 18th century such nations as Portugal, Spain, and the Netherlands wielded tremendous influence in world politics. Gradually these maritime nations were eclipsed by countries of larger resources and more advanced technology. It may be that the introduction of western civilization to the Orient has set in motion a similar evolution. If so, we may expect that the vast population of India, at present untrained and not firmly united, will grow in technical skill and social capa-

---

[8] Based on United Nations, *Statistical Yearbook, 1954,* Table 36.

bility.   As the proficiency for large unified efforts increases, India may well rise in a few decades to the ranks of the super powers through processes of growth similar to those that have caused other countries to ascend rapidly in the scale of economic potential.

THE VALUE OF THE ECONOMIC POTENTIAL CONCEPT IN ATOMIC WAR

Each spring when the Industrial College of the Armed Forces begins its study of the subject of economic potential, the question is raised as to whether the economic potential concept has any value today.   A nuclear war, it is pointed out, may last but a few weeks and the major decision of the conflict may be made before the economic resources of the country can be converted to war purposes—a process which takes about two years.   In a short war the only resources that will have any effect on the decision are those that are already converted into munitions on D-Day.   In view of these facts, some questioner will invariably ask, why should the subject of economic potential for war receive any consideration ?

It must be admitted that a nation's economic potential for war does not now appear to have value in the same form as it did before the coming of nuclear weapons.   In each of the previous World Wars there was a long waiting period of more than two years before the United States entered the war.   There ensued another period of many months before American troops had large-scale contact with the enemy. The time available for converting economic potential into actual war strength was thus considerable.   We may assume that there will be no such period in a future war.   Notice of such a war may come when at some far northern early-warning station the images of a number of fast-moving planes are seen on the radar scope and an excited message is relayed to Washington that the attack has begun.   The battle of nuclear weapons may be over before the major contracts for munitions can even be signed.

If the value of economic potential will not be in its conversion for major combat after a war has begun, there are still some situations in which it is of great importance, perhaps greater than in the past. In the preparatory period before a war starts, the economic potential of a nation will determine the strength of its efforts in making ready for an actual test of nuclear weapons.   During this period some types of preparations will exceed those of previous all-out wars.   Not only must munitions be produced, but an effort to solve the problems of science on a much greater scale than at present should be made. Friendly nations must be supported to enable them to remain in the ranks of the free nations.   All of these efforts require the conversion of great economic potential. A country which is weak in human and natural resources could not rate high in this period of competition. Even after the beginning of a nuclear war the military effort will be dragged out for many years following the major decision. If the United States should win the opening and decisive phase of such a war, we would have to expect a protracted period of pacification, restoration of order, and establishment of a world organization that would prevent future attacks. Such an effort would require the backing of great economic resources. In this period there would be time for the conversion of potential which would have been denied in the opening phase of the war. Altogether, if peace does not come and the world staggers on toward a crescendo of bitter combat, the competition between the powers will be grueling. The existence of economic resources and the ability to make proper use of them will continue to be one of the chief deciding factors.[9]

---

[9] For a similar opinion on the continued importance of economic potential see Knorr, Klaus, Chapter V, in Kaufmann, William W. (ed.), *Military Policy and National Security,* Princeton, N. J., Princeton University Press, 1956.

IV
GOVERNMENT CONTROLS IN ECONOMIC MOBILIZATION

Statistical data of the kind presented in preceding chapters tell only part of the story, and in many respects the simplest part. As we advanced from the late eighteenth to the twentieth century, the problems of mobilizing the productive resources of the nation in support of a full-scale war become more and more complex. They cannot be met simply by increasing the scale and the speed of the recruitment of men, the procurement of supplies, and the financial measures to provide the funds to pay for both. Increasingly the government finds it necessary to intervene actively in the operation of the economic system, exercising a variety of control measures bearing directly upon the functioning of the economic system. These include materials controls, manpower controls, export and import controls, credit controls, and, in some respects the most pervasive of all controls, price controls.

THE EXAMPLE OF PRICE CONTROL

The action of the government in the stabilization of prices furnishes an excellent example of economic controls. In every major war, the rapid rise in the level of prices—inflation—has had very disturbing effects, not only upon the conduct of business and upon the productivity of industry but upon the national morale. During the Revolution, the issue of large quantities of paper money as a financial expedient led to inflation and to the depreciation of the money to the point where it was all but worthless. During the Civil War, also, inflation resulting from the issue of large quantities of paper money by both the Federal and Confederate governments added materially to the difficulties of prosecuting the war. In the case of the South, the financial difficulties and the civilian demoralization associated with monetary inflation were a major cause of the collapse of the Confederacy. Not until World War I was any effective effort made to control inflation, and not until World War II was a separate agency established to administer price controls.

But why is the control of prices in wartime so essential? Simply because under the pressure of a vast armament program the demand for materials, products, facilities, and labor involved in the produc-

	REVOLUTIONARY WAR	CIVIL WAR FEDERAL	CIVIL WAR CONFEDERACY	WORLD WAR I	WORLD WAR II
RENT					▦
WAGE					▦
PROFIT					▦
CREDIT				▦	▦
MANPOWER			◢		▦
RATIONING			◢	◢	▦
MATERIALS			◢	▦	▦
PRICE	◢		◢	▦	▦
EXPORT		◢	◢	▦	▦
MONETARY	▦	▦	▦	▦	▦

◢ CONTROLS USED IN A LIMITED WAY   ▦ MAJOR CONTROLS

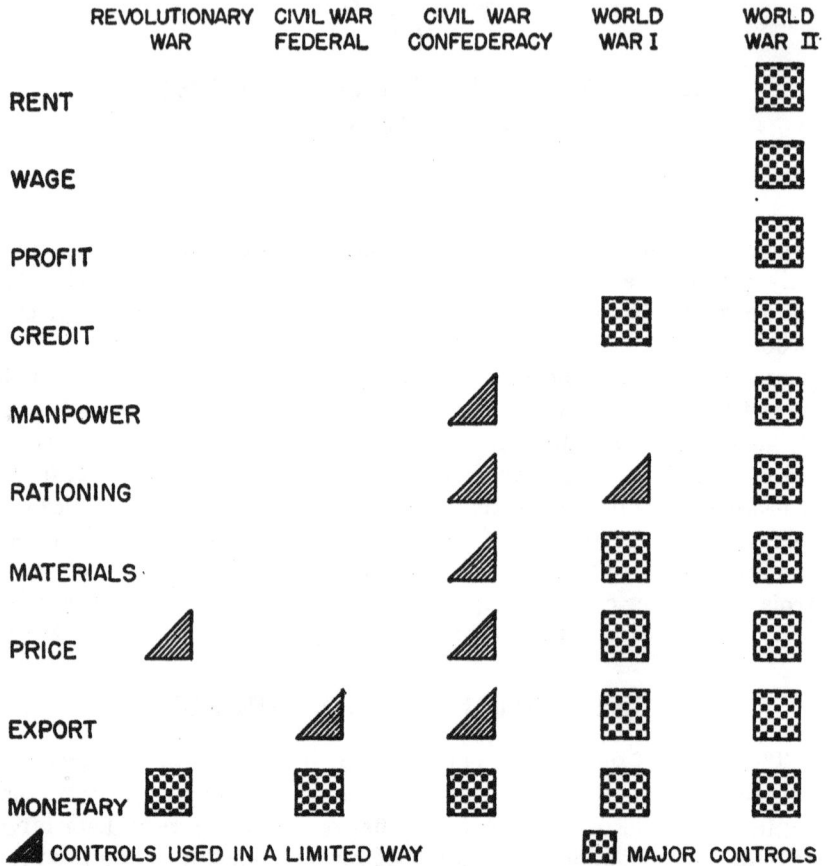

Figure 2. Economic controls exercised by the government in wartime.

tion of munitions is so tremendous as to be virtually unlimited. The supply of these things, on the other hand, is limited by productive capacity, and this can be increased but slowly. To build and equip new plants—steel mills, oil refineries, textile mills, aircraft plants, and scores of others—takes many months and by absorbing large quantities of materials and manpower further accentuates growing scarcities. If uncontrolled this unbalance between supply and demand will lead to a gradually accelerating upward spiral of prices with inflation assuming increasingly serious proportions.

Cost-price relationships are vital at every level of business and industry. As costs go up, so must prices; and since one man's prices become the next man's costs and add to the charges for his products, prices take an upward spiral course. Some individuals—particularly speculators—can take advantage of inflation and profit by it.

But production almost invariably will suffer, and it is on production that the armed forces depend for much of their fighting strength. Manufacturers are worried lest rising costs wipe out profits on existing contracts and are fearful of taking new contracts lest these, too, result in losses rather than gains.

Calculations of costs are continually upset by further price increases. No one can be certain of what the future holds. Workers become dissatisfied with take-home dollars that put less and less in the take-home market basket. Fixed income groups suffer from a rising price level which results in falling purchasing power. The knowledge that many are profiting from the speculative opportunities provided by inflationary conditions embitters and demoralizes those who suffer from mounting prices. For these reasons the Government has taken the unusual step of controlling prices as well as credit and wages. The details of these actions will be described in a subsequent volume.

THE RECENT REVOLUTION IN ECONOMIC MOBILIZATION

During the last three generations, warfare has become increasingly identified with, and dependent upon, the exercise of controls by the Government over the operation of the economic system. Figure 2 presents in simplified form a summary view of the increasing resort to control measures in wartime. It reveals very effectively the increasing complexity of the task of mobilizing the productive resources of a nation for war. Not only has the imposition of such controls on economic life not been welcome in this country, they have in each instance been adopted only with great reluctance and with a grudging recognition that there has been no alternative to their acceptance, much as they have been disliked by the American people.

The first World War marks a significant turning point in the history of economic mobilization. It demonstrated to all the belligerent powers that the traditional methods of meeting the supply requirements of armed forces were quite inadequate for dealing with the novel conditions of mechanized mass conflict. It was discovered during the first year of the war that the old formula of men, money and munitions, supplied by conscription, by taxation, and loans, and by the expansion of peacetime procurement methods, respectively, was incapable of providing the necessary military strength. New and drastic measures had to be adopted by the belligerents in order to obtain munitions in the unprecedentedly great quantities demanded by the new mechanized warfare—a warfare employing for the first time on a large scale the machine gun, the rapid-fire field gun and the submarine, and introducing the automobile, the airplane, and the tank.

Both land and sea warfare was conducted on a scale and with an intensity that dwarfed all previous military operations. Armies of millions of men extending along fronts hundreds of miles in length were in continuous contact; and, in the periodic efforts of the opposing forces to break the stalemate of trench warfare by mass offensives, tremendous quantities of shells, ammunition, and other supplies were expended.

In the United States the traditional method of procuring military supplies in wartime was by contracting in the open market with manufacturers and other suppliers. So long as armies and navies were small, equipment simple and easy to manufacture, and expenditures of munitions low, open-market procurement gave reasonably satisfactory results. The impact of military procurement upon industry and the economy was relatively small. In the new mechanized warfare, involving mass armies, this was no longer the case. Equipment and supply requirements were vastly greater in amount; they involved far more numerous, complex, and costly items than in previous wars. In contrast with the equipment and weapons of the past, many basic types of new military equipment were intricate mechanisms, built to exacting standards of precision and durability. Many of them had no civilian counterparts and in peacetime had been produced only in small quantities or not at all.

Finally, the time factor assumed a critical importance as never before. So evenly balanced were the contending forces that the side which could place additional units in the field would have a big advantage. No longer was the limiting factor the time required to recruit and train men but rather the time required to produce the weapons and materiel for their equipment. Even with the great resources of American industry, the experience of World War I demonstrated that from 12 to 24 months were required to get a new major weapon such as a field gun, aircraft, or tank into quantity production. The conversion of a factory from its normal product to one of the simpler types of military material often required from six to twelve months. So great was the lag in armament production that the American Expeditionary Forces were dependent for many important major items of equipment upon our Allies.

In the Second World War the problems of economic mobilization were fundamentally very similar to those of World War I, but the magnitude and complexity of the economic forces to be directed and controlled were far greater. Mechanization of combat and supply was carried much further than in the earlier conflict. The numbers engaged were far greater, and the theaters of operation were more numerous and more widely dispersed. The war itself was of longer duration, extending, for the United States, more than twice as long as in 1917–1918.

The prosecution of warfare on a global scale placed an unprecedented burden not only upon individual productive resources, such as industrial facilities, manpower, and transportation, but also upon the economic system as a working whole. In the case of the nations most fully committed in the war against the Axis—Great Britain and the U. S. S. R.—one-half of the total national income was devoted to the prosecution of the war. This was an extraordinary and unprecedented achievement itself.

Moreover, the national income was increased far above the levels achieved in the best peactime years.. For example, in the United States the national income (the total value of the goods and services produced in the nation annually) rose from 81 billion dollars in 1940 to 182 billions in 1944. Even when allowance is made for the rise in the general price level, these figures represent a fifty percent increase in a period of four years. An increase of this magnitude was a tribute not only to the extraordinary productive efficiency of the American economy but also to the organizational and administrative skills required to transform this economy into a great war-making machine.

THE PLANNED AND CONTROLLED ECONOMY OF WARTIME

With the experience of two World Wars behind us, the character and objectives of economic mobilization have become clear enough. The scale, the intensity, and the duration of any military effort are dependent upon the ability of the nation's economic system to supply the manpower, the materials, and the munitions required to establish and maintain armed forces. The mobilization of the nation's productive resources aims not only at the maximum conversion of these resources from peacetime to military uses but also at the greatest possible expansion of war-supporting production. And in both the conversion and expansion of production, time is the critical element. General Forrest's homely prescription for victory—to "git thar fustest with the mostest"—is as sound today as it was during the Civil War. From the experience of two World Wars we have learned much regarding the major difficulties to be overcome and the major problems to be solved if a rapid and effective mobilization of the economic system for war is to be carried out.

One major lesson of these wars is that the character and functioning of the economy itself must be changed in important respects if the tremendous load placed on the economy by wartime requirements is to be carried. In the peacetime economy, freedom of choice and decision on the part of all concerned—manufacturer and businessman, worker and farmer, producer and consumer—are characteristic of the functioning of the "free enterprise system." Experience has demonstrated clearly that this freedom of choice must be restricted in important respects if maximum production is to be obtained under wartime conditions. The war economy is, in fact, to a considerable degree a planned and controlled economy, an economic system directed and coordinated from Washington. An elaborate system of controls is imposed: controls over materials, over prices, wages and profits, over production, over manpower. To administer and coordinate these controls so as to attain maximum war production presents what are in many respects the most difficult problems of economic mobilization.

V

THE PARTS OF THE PROCESS OF ECONOMIC MOBILIZATION

With this general review of the character and development of economic mobilization, we are ready to analyze the subject in terms of its component parts and to consider briefly some of the major components in turn.

THE STRATEGIC PLAN

Since the purpose of economic mobilization is to provide the supply or logistical support for military operations, any program of economic mobilization takes its departure from the strategic plan. The strategic plan defines the military objectives of an impending or existing war and the ways and means proposed for attaining these objectives. The theaters of operations, the character and scale of military operations in each, the number, kind, and size of military units required, and the time schedule are all indicated in the strategic plan.

THE DETERMINATION OF REQUIREMENTS

The strategic plan provides the basis for taking the first step in economic mobilization, namely, determining requirements: requirements in men, in equipment, in supplies and in all that is necessary to train, equip, transport, and maintain armed forces in the field, in support of the operational plans. Calculating the number of men, planes, tanks, ships, guns, uniforms, and the hundreds of other military end items is in itself a complex, difficult, and time consuming task. But this is only the first step in requirements determination. The supply branches of the armed services must carry the process a step further. They must calculate the number of productive facilities, the amount of raw materials—aluminum, steel, copper—and the number of critical components—anti-friction bearings, fractional horsepower motors, heat exchangers—required for the production of the required military end items.

To military requirements must be added what are called foreign aid requirements—all the goods, equipment, materials, etc., that in wartime we shall need to supply to our allies and to those neutral countries we find it expedient to aid.

Finally, it is necessary to determine what is required to keep the civilian population and essential civilian industries and services in a state of productive efficiency. In some respects this is the most perplexing problem of all because it is so difficult to determine where to draw the line between what people would like to have and what they actually must have if they are to work at the highest level of efficiency. It is easy to say that under the conditions of a war crisis civilians and industries and services should make drastic sacrifices for the common cause; but how drastic a reduction in standard of living and in materials for repair, maintenance, and replacement of plant and equipment can be made without impairing productive efficiency of the entire economy? For example, a few persons would be inclined to argue that such things as bobby pins, lipstick, soft drinks and movies are indispensable to an all-out war effort. Yet their availability will have an effect upon civilian morale and thereby upon productivity which cannot safely be ignored.

BALANCING REQUIREMENTS AND RESOURCES

If war requirements—military, foreign aid, civilian—are to be realistic, they must be related to the basic resources and productive capacity of the national economy. It would be simple for the Armed Forces to adopt a strategic plan calling, say, for 25 million men, 100,000 heavy bombers, and other equipment and supplies in proportion. If, however, materiel and men simply cannot be provided in such quantities, strategic plans based on the assumption of their availability will be of little value. The requirements of strategic plans and the productive capacity of the nation must be made to balance. If productive capacity cannot be increased sufficiently to meet requirements, then the strategic plans must be modified to the point where the men and materiel for their execution can be supplied. The resources-requirements balance is a basic essential in sound economic mobilization.

PROCUREMENT

Once requirements for military items have been determined in accordance with the strategic plans, consolidated with foreign aid and civilian requirements, and brought into balance with overall productive capacity, the next step in economic mobilization is procurement.

In the United States, responsibility for the procurement of all military equipment and supplies has long rested with the armed services. Each service designs and develops its own weapons and equipment, from the research on which the concept of the new item is based through the development, testing, and final approval of the item for use. Procurement includes not only purchase—the letting of contracts for the items required—but also the supervision of the execution of the contract, inspection of the finished items, packaging and transportation, and the storage and issue by the using service.

Under normal peacetime conditions, such as prevailed between 1919 and 1939, when the armed services are maintained on a relatively small scale, the problems of procurement are relatively simple. The amounts required are not large, manufacturers are usually eager to obtain military contracts, competitive bidding is keen, materials and manpower are plentiful, and the time factor is not an urgent one. All this is abruptly changed when a war emergency becomes imminent. As the armed services mushroom from a few hundred thousand men to five, ten, or more millions, total military expenditures multiply in even greater proportion and are measured not in tens or hundreds of millions of dollars but in billions. Everyone is trying to get more of everything. Raw materials, facilities, industrial equipment, and manpower in turn become scarce. Procurement operations not only expand tremendously in quantity but they encounter increasing difficulties. The time element becomes a critical factor.

PRODUCTION

Production is the axis about which the war economy turns and upon which the scale and effectiveness of the war effort depend. Production includes not only the fabrication of direct military equipment and supplies and of essential civilian goods of all kinds, it covers the provision of equipment for essential services such as transportation, communications and power as well. It includes, of course, provision of the supplies of basic raw materials on which all industry depends.

War production differs from peacetime production in several important respects. It is, in the first place, all-out, maximum production, attaining levels much higher than those even of prosperity booms in peacetime. It is production with virtually all the slack removed, operating with expanded capacity, longer hours, and multiple shifts.

Secondly, war production calls not only for greatly expanded capacity but for capacity converted from the production of the familiar articles of peacetime to the production of the unfamiliar, highly complicated materiel of war. It demands working to standards of quality and precision much higher than those necessary or desirable in most civilian products.

Thirdly, considerations of financial cost are of secondary importance in war production; quality of product and speed of production come first. The vital costs in war production are not costs reckoned in dollars and cents, which can be met without too great difficulty by taxation and government borrowing, but costs measured in labor, materials, and equipment.

Finally, war production is production that is planned, directed, and controlled by national authority to meet national objectives; it is production geared to strategic plans and coordinated by legislatively established policies administered by a galaxy of Federal agencies. The decisions as to what is made, in what amounts, and in what order, for whom, and at what price, are in the main those of Government and not of individual business men and consumers. The profit motive and the incentives of higher wage or salary incomes are retained, but are subjected to restrictions and limitations.

The direction and coordination of wartime production is exercised by the Government through a variety of production controls. The most fundamental of these are the controls over the raw materials upon which all production depends. Under authority granted by Congress, raw materials in critically short supply are distributed among producers in the order of importance of their products in the war production program. The key questions to be answered in a war production materials program are: Who gets what, how much, and in what order of priority? To supply the answers to these questions, for hundreds of industries and tens of thousands of companies, is the full-time task of many thousands of government employees, servicing vast numbers of requests embodied in a mountain of paper work. Elaborate systems of priority are devised to facilitate materials distribution, employing preference ratings, allocations, and other devices. Direct controls are established over materials in other ways by such means as limitations upon inventories, prohibition of the use of materials for certain purposes (automobiles, for example), and restriction of the materials allowed for use in certain products.

Controls over raw materials are supplemented by controls over machinery and equipment (such as machine tools), over end products (such as tires and trucks), and over other essential materials (such as fuel). Still other controls are concerned directly with the management of production as in the case of production scheduling which directs the manufacturer in what order, in what amounts, and for what customers specified articles are to be produced.

As labor shortages appear and spread, it becomes essential to devise and apply controls over manpower which will direct this vital element in production to the industries, the regions, and the manufacturers where it is most needed to advance war production. Strikes and other impediments to production resulting from unsatisfactory labor-management relations lead sooner or later in wartime to government intervention to an extent that would hardly prove acceptable in peacetime.

Still another type of control over production is that which involves the granting of subsidies, direct or indirect, to certain classes of producers, such as small business concerns, and marginal (high cost) mines, and to producers of critical agricultural products.

ECONOMIC STABILIZATION

Direct and indirect controls over production of the kind mentioned above are not enough in themselves to insure maximum and balanced production of essential goods required for a major war effort. Production, after all, operates within the larger framework of the economic system. The effect of general economic conditions upon production is illustrated in peacetime by the sensitive response of industrial output to market changes and by the close relations between production levels and general business conditions.

One of the most revealing differences between peacetime and wartime economies is the circumstance that, while peacetime producers operate most of the time in a buyers' market, the chronic condition of wartime is one of a sellers' market. From the very nature of things, supply cannot keep up with demand, and the continued and often wide gap between the two is a persistent threat to the stability of the economic system as a whole. Under peacetime conditions in a free enterprise system, the problem of a scarcity is met through the flow of capital, managerial skill, and labor from the areas of less active demand—where profits, wages, and salaries are lower—to areas of more active demand—where the returns are higher. The result is a tendency toward balance, or equilibrium, in the market.

Under conditions of wartime, shortages are too general and too great for a balance between supply and demand to be reached. Without government intervention, the natural market forces will produce an upward spiraling of prices ending in a galloping inflation with disturbing repercussions on every phase of the economy. Price control, as has been stated in chapter IV, is essential for maintaining the economic stability which, as we have seen is so essential to the conduct of orderly business relations, the maintenance of business confidence and the support of public morale.

In the broadest sense, of course, price control includes not only control of prices of goods, commodities and services but control of profits, wages, and rents.

Price control is only one of the measures employed to give stability to an economic system running at high speed and subject to extraordinary disturbing influences. While consumer goods are becoming increasingly scarce, due to restrictions on production of less essential goods, mass purchasing power is rising steadily. This rise takes place in response not only to higher wages but even more to increased employment, longer hours, and overtime pay. Family incomes rise sharply as women and older children join the working force. Personal incomes of professional and salaried groups and from business profits are likewise moving upward and adding to the amount of disposable funds.

This higher consumer income exerts a powerful inflationary pressure on markets as civilian workers seek to spend their money. Taxation measures, rationing of scarce essential goods, and voluntary savings programs are among the more important devices employed by the Government to contain the inflationary influences of higher incomes. In sum, the wide gap between supply and demand, which is a major characteristic of the wartime economy, creates a condition of unbalance which, if uncontrolled, will have a disturbing and demoralizing influence on every phase of production. The Government must supply artificially the stability which the economy itself, under the abnormal conditions of war, cannot provide.

THE ORGANIZATION OF ECONOMIC MOBILIZATION

The shift from a private enterprise economy of peacetime, in which the Government plays a relatively minor role, to the planned and directed economy of wartime is one of extraordinary difficulty. Virtually overnight free enterprise is, in many important respects, supplanted by government. The decisions of individual business men, within the framework of a competitive economy, are in many vital issues, replaced by or subordinated to the decisions of governmental officials. In effect, the Government assumes responsibility for the direction and coordination of the vast and interdependent productive resources of a highly industrialized nation of 160 million people.

In carrying out this tremendous task, not only is there little experience to provide guidance and direction but the necessity of making the changeover with the utmost speed adds greatly to the difficulties inherent in the process. The strain placed on the organizational and administrative resources of a government which has developed in response to the quite different needs of peacetime is very great.

In each World War, the United States has been faced with the same basic problem of developing the organizational arrangements and devising the administrative policies and procedures requisite for performing the functions of economic direction and control.

To some extent the established government agencies can expand and convert their organizations to meet the necessities of a national emergency. For the most part, however, the problem of administering the numerous wartime controls has in both wars been solved by the creation of new "war" or "emergency" agencies. Even under the simpler conditions of World War I literally scores of new agencies were set up in Washington to wrestle with the innumerable difficulties met with in the process of adapting the nation's economic life to wartime needs. Major agencies were established to deal with problems of mobilizing industry, labor, transportation and communications, fuel, food products, aircraft construction, foreign trade, finance, and publicity. These were supplemented by numerous other agencies concerned with lesser though necessary governmental functions of wartime.

World War II saw a repetition of World War I but on a larger and more intensive scale. The number of specially created war agencies was probably smaller; but, in the scale and complexity of their operations, these agencies quite overshadowed those of the earlier war. Federal employees of the Executive Branch rose from less than a million in 1939 to 3.8 millions at the peak of war employment in 1945. Some 70 percent of these were in the War and Navy Departments. The number in the special war establishments was 173,000. The American economy was more fully committed in the Second than in the First World War. The strain on our productive resources was greater, the controls more numerous and more tightly administered, and the problems of coordinating the activities of the various agencies more complicated.

With separate agencies set up to handle production, price control, manpower, transportation, and other key functions, the problem of coordinating these functions to prevent duplication, overlapping, competition, and conflict was a very serious one, a problem, indeed, that was never fully resolved down to the end of hostilities. Indeed, judged by the evidence of newspaper headlines, the administrative battles fought on the Washington front appeared to be scarcely of a lesser magnitude and bitterness than those waged in the overseas theaters.

Unquestionably the mobilization of a complex industrial economy for modern war presents administrative and organizational problems of the first order. This is particularly true in a nation with a democratic system of government and with an economy which in peacetime operates with relatively limited intervention from government authority.

HOW BIG A WAR LOAD CAN THE ECONOMY CARRY?

As pointed out earlier, the cost of waging war has risen tremendously during the past 150 years, and especially during the past generation. The load placed by modern war on the economic systems of some countries was so great in World War I as to hasten their military defeat. Even an economy as strong as that of Great Britain would have found it difficult to avoid collapse had not the United States come to its aid with credit and loans on a large scale in World War I and again with lend-lease in World War II. The extraordinary fact of American experience in World War II was the ease with which the economic system carried the burden of vast military requirements and at the same time actually enabled the civilian population to raise its standard of living, enjoying a steadily rising level of expenditures for goods and services. In the popular phrase, large segments of the civilian population never had it so good. From 1940 to 1945 total population rose 6 percent but during these same war years consumer expenditures rose 20 percent, in spite of the fact that the stoppage or drastic reduction of production of such durable goods as automobiles, refrigerators, and the like limited expenditures for these much desired goods.

This rise in consumer expenditures and in the civilian standard of living took place in the face of military expenditures which are indicated in table 9. In 1944, as can be seen from the table, expenditures for national security were almost equal to those for the personal consumption of the American people, being about 90 percent.

What made possible the remarkable achievements in both military and civilian expenditures? The answer is found in the unprecedented—and unparalleled—increase in the productivity and total output of the American economic system. The total value of goods and services produced in the United States—the gross national product measured in constant (1952) dollars as shown in column 2—rose from the depression low of 120 billion dollars in 1933 to 202 billions in 1940. It then mounted to a peak of 324 billion dollars in 1944, a 60 percent

Table 9. *Performance of the American Economy Before and During World War II*

[Billions of dollars at 1952 prices]

Year	Population	Gross national product	Personal consumption expenditures	Gross private investment	National security expenditures
1929	121, 800, 000	172. 5	121. 6	33. 7	(1)
1933	125, 600, 000	120. 5	99. 3	3. 7	(1)
1940	132, 000, 000	202. 1	140. 6	30. 2	4. 8
1941	133, 200, 000	234. 9	151. 5	37. 5	24. 9
1942	134, 700, 000	266. 5	149. 3	20. 4	80. 5
1943	136, 500, 000	300. 2	153. 2	11. 6	126. 5
1944	138, 000, 000	323. 7	159. 5	13. 7	142. 3
1945	139, 600, 000	314. 1	170. 0	17. 0	119. 2

1 Not available.

increase in a five-year period.   During these same years, 1940–44, national security expenditures—military service, foreign aid, atomic energy, civil defense, etc., column 5, rose from about 5 billion dollars to 142 billions or from 2.4 to 44 percent of the gross national product. In other words, we provided the means for fighting the war largely out of the great increase in the productive output of the nation.

In relating the experience of World War II to the war supporting capabilities of the American economy in a possible future world conflict, several points should be noted.   At the beginning of the upsurge in gross national product in 1940, the economy was operating substantially below full capacity, with over 8 million workers unemployed. Since 1945 the economy has been working close to capacity most of the time, leaving little slack to be taken up in the event of a national emergency.   Second, in World War II, the United States, unlike its major allies, experienced no damage from enemy action, whether by ground or air forces, on its own territory.   In the new age of atomic air warfare, the possibility of heavy damage to productive facilities from atomic attack, with consequent loss of production, must be assumed. Third, while it is not possible to determine with any precision minimum civilian consumption requirements in a future emergency, there is no doubt that the civilian population, should conditions require it, could get along with a much lower level of consumer goods and services than was enjoyed in World War II.   The maintenance of the civilian economy on an austerity level would allow a materially greater diversion of productive resources from civilian to military needs than was the case in World War II.   In the last analysis, how big a load the American economy can bear in a future war will depend to a significant degree upon the morale and unity of the people and upon their willingness to accept material deprivations in the interest of national survival.

PLANNING FOR ECONOMIC MOBILIZATION

It is possible in a totalitarian regime to maintain the economy on a near war footing even in peacetime.   If industry is government owned or subject to close government direction at all times, the problems of placing the economy on a war basis are greatly simplified. The administrative machinery for directing the productive resources— manufacturing, labor, transportation and the rest—is already in being; it remains only for this machinery to be thrown into high gear and brought up to maximum speed.

In nations having democratic governments, especially where the system of private enterprise rules, and where the peacetime military establishment is maintained on a quite limited scale, the problems of economic mobilization are difficult. The smaller the armed forces in peacetime and the more limited the normal role of government in economic life, the harder is the task of placing the nation on a war basis. The problems of expanding the military establishments many-fold overnight for waging mass warfare are very serious; those of transforming the productive resources of the nation into one vast coordinated arsenal are even more serious.

In a democracy the alternative to a permanently mobilized economy is planning. Planning for economic mobilization in the United States dates from the end of World War I. The National Defense Act of 1920, reorganizing the military establishment in the light of World War I experiences, placed responsibility for "the assurance of adequate provision for mobilization of material and industrial organizations essential to wartime needs" upon the Assistant Secretary of War. A Planning Branch was early established in the Office of the Assistant Secretary to carry on the planning work. The Army and Navy Munitions Board was formed by interservice agreement to coordinate industrial mobilization planning within the military establishment, and, in 1924, an Army Industrial College was set up to instruct officers in all matters relating to military procurement and industrial mobilization in wartime.

Planning activities continued throughout the between-wars period. The most publicized results of this planning were a series of "industrial mobilization plans," the last of which was published in the fall of 1939 after the war in Europe had begun. The 1939 plan was a published Government document of less than twenty pages; it was supplemented and expanded at considerable length by a series of unpublished "annexes," each dealing with specific phases of economic mobilization. The organizational plan itself was never put into effect in any formal sense for a variety of reasons which are still a subject of some controversy. Some valuable concepts for "industrial mobilization" were, however, developed. Those of stockpiling, negotiated contracts, and the allocation of industrial facilities may be mentioned. They have long since become part of the standard operating procedure in economic mobilization.

The experience of the Second World War, combined with dissatisfaction with planning activities as conducted during the prewar years, led to a reorganization of economic mobilization planning following the war. This was done under the authority of the National Security Act of 1947, revised in 1949. A new civilian agency, the National Security Resources Board, responsible directly to the President, was given the duty of overall planning for economic mobilization; and a Munitions Board—in effect a strengthened and much enlarged Army and

Navy Munitions Board—was established to plan for the military aspects of industrial mobilization.   In sum, economic mobilization planning was given a broader base, placed at a higher level in the chain of command, and given general recognition as a major phase in the structure of national security.

In December 1950, shortly after the outbreak of the Korean war, the Office of Defense Mobilization was established for the purpose of directing and coordinating economic mobilization activities.   The existence of two planning agencies—NSRB which advised on plans for the future and ODM which directed and coordinated current planning—seemed a duplication.   In 1953 NSRB was abolished and its functions transferred to ODM.   Shortly afterward the Munitions Board was eliminated and its duties shifted to the Office of the Secretary of Defense, in which establishment they are administered by the Assistant Secretary of Defense (Supply and Logistics).   The burden of the work is currently proceeding there much as it was under the Munitions Board.

Particular emphasis has been given by the planning agencies to what is termed the resources-requirements balance sheet so that the Government will know at all times just where it stands in respect both to military and civilian requirements in another war and to the ability of the economy to produce these requirements to meet the conditions of strategic plans for conducting war if war comes.

Another aspect of planning focuses attention upon the major problems and problem areas which will be present in a future economic mobilization.   Attention is fixed not only upon the difficulties experienced in previous wars which may reasonably be expected to recur but also, and of particular importance, upon new problems and difficulties which will arise from changing conditions and developments, political, technical, and economic, and on which past experience can throw little light and provide little guidance.   Moreover, the emphasis in planning tends to be placed first on what has to be done to mobilize the economy; secondly, what policies and procedures are essential for the attainment of this objective; and, finally, what agencies shall be established to administer these policies and by what means will the work of these agencies be coordinated.

PARTIAL OR FULL MOBILIZATION

One problem that has plagued both the planners and directors of economic mobilization is the scope and the scale of the mobilization effort.   In the 1930's, planning was directed to the believed requirements of all-out war, which, it was assumed, would begin on a specific date (M-Day or Mobilization Day) with a declaration of war.   One of the reasons for the failure to adopt the Industrial Mobilization Plan, which was the principal end product of planning before 1939, was the gradual manner in which the United States became involved in the war over an 18-month period between May 1940 and December 1941. Between 1945 and the outbreak of the Korean war in June 1950, likewise, much of the economic mobilization planning was in terms of an all-out war which, in the belief of many, would begin with an air attack with atomic weapons.

The outbreak of war in Korea marked the beginning, not of all-out economic mobilization for total war but of partial mobilization for a war of limited objectives. As the war in Korea continued, it became increasingly apparent that even if this war were brought to an end, a full demobilization of military and economic resources, such as took place in 1946 and 1947, would not be possible.

The course of economic mobilization since June 1950 has increasingly been based on the assumption that the United States must be prepared to maintain both its military forces and the economic resources supporting them, on a high level of preparedness for the eventuality of a possible all-out war. In view of the continuing threat to world peace presented by the U. S. S. R. and associated Communist regimes in other countries, a partial or limited, mobilization of military resources of the United States is in prospect for an indefinite period in the future. Such a partial mobilization of economic resources for limited warfare or for defense, presents problems that are different both in character and in scale from those which this nation has faced in the past. The differences between partial mobilization and a full-scale effort will be discussed in a later volume.

ECONOMIC MOBILIZATION AND ATOMIC WARFARE

The introduction of atomic weapons, the tremendous increase in their destructive capabilities, and their growing availability for use by each of the major power blocs raise questions of great significance for economic mobilization. Some have argued that atomic warfare has made both the concept and practice of economic mobilization obsolete. Clearly the scope and the character of the economic problems of supporting war have been seriously affected.

There is little doubt that each of the two leading military powers in the world has a sufficient number of atomic weapons and of planes for their delivery to direct simultaneous attacks with devastating destructiveness upon as many as 50 or more urban and industrial centers of an enemy nation. It is quite within the range of probability that, as a result of such massive atomic attack, the destruction of life and of property would be such as to paralyze for an indefinite time the economic and political life of the nation. The direct losses in human life and industrial facilities and services would be on a colossal scale. Tens of millions of deaths would result, and conceivably as much as one-fourth to one-third of the productive capacity of the nation would be destroyed outright. The requirements for the care of the millions of sick and injured and for the hordes of evacuees from the metropolitan areas affected would place a tremendous burden on the rest of the nation.

There would be more than the direct losses to consider. The repercussive effects of the personnel losses and property destruction upon the functioning of a highly interdependent, complex, and delicately balanced economy might well bring the entire productive system of the nation to something approaching a standstill. It has, indeed, been argued with force that the effect of the initial massive attack with atomic weapons might be to reduce the nations affected to a level at which maintenance of the remaining population on a bare survival basis would tax the material and institutional resources left intact. If these views are well-founded, an all-out atomic war would probably be of short duration. Neither side would be able to do much beyond delivering the initial and retaliatory blows. A few weeks or at most several months would find the belligerent powers reduced to a condition of military impotence.

What place would economic mobilization have in an atomic war initiated with such devastating suddenness and producing such catastrophic consequences? Experience can throw little light on this question; the mass bombings of World War II appear almost trivial when compared with the super-Hiroshimas of which military destructiveness is now capable. The problem falls largely within the realm of speculation. Here it is possible only to suggest certain alternative lines of thought.

One view holds that under the conditions of massive atomic attack there would be neither the occasion nor the opportunity to mobilize the resources of the economy in support of the war. The initial atomic strikes together with such lesser ones as might be expected to follow, would bring a decision or a condition of paralytic stalemate within a matter of weeks, or at most several months. But experience has shown that many months are required to mobilize the economic resources of a nation such as ours, even under favorable conditions. Therefore an atomic war would have to be fought, and won or lost, with the military forces and weapons *in being* at the time of the initial onslaught. Economic mobilization plans and readiness measures would have no meaning since a military decision would have been reached and the combat phase of the war over before they could be made operative. If the foregoing view is sound, the outcome of atomic wars between great powers would not be determined, as in the last two great world conflicts, by the economic resources and capabilities of the belligerents and by the skill displayed in converting these capabilities fully and rapidly to war purposes.

Such a conclusion, however probable, is not inescapable. Once the initial and devastating shock of atomic conflict was past, the will to fight might persist on both sides. With recovery from the immediate paralysis, the opposing forces would muster what resources they could for the resumption of the conflict. What has been termed a "broken back war" might ensue with combat limited to the capabilities of hand weapons and the simpler types of military equipment and to military forces of quite modest size. Under the conditions of physical devastation and economic disruption, the support of even a "broken back war" would present great difficulties, since minimal provisions for the care of the sick and injured and for physical rehabilitation would place a tremendous load on the gravely weakened economy. Extraordinary measures for the direction and control of economic resources by government—Federal, State, and municipal—could hardly be avoided. The mobilization of the economy would doubtless require very different expedients and follow a different course from those of previous national emergencies. For a time, at least, such mobilization might be closer to the experience of the Confederacy in the Civil War than to that of World War II; but it would be economic mobilization nonetheless. The imperative to mobilize would be even greater with disaster on a vast scale in our midst than when, as in earlier conflicts, it was thousands of miles removed overseas.

Other possible alternatives may be briefly considered. Atomic warfare might be either *more* devastating, or *less* devastating than pictured above. Or, as a result of formal or tacit agreement among the great powers, the use of atomic weapons might be limited to tactical purposes, to the exclusion of civilian, particularly urban and industrial, targets.

If atomic warfare was *more* devastating, the will to continue the war, to say nothing of the means, might well be lacking. Yet the requirements of recovery, rehabilitation, and reconstruction would be so tremendous that governmental planning, direction, and control of the economy, whether on a local, state, regional and/or national basis, would be inescapable. The demands of peace would hardly be less imperative than those of war. The mobilization of the surviving economic resources would be indispensable, not simply to speed the work of recovery but to prevent chaos. Instead of mobilization for defense or war, we would be confronted with the necessity of economic mobilization for survival—and possibly on a permanent basis.

Similarly, if, following a short but devastating atomic struggle, the enemy should surrender, leaving this nation with the formidable task of establishing and maintaining international order, the compulsion to mobilize economically on a world as well as a national basis would seem unavoidable. If, on the other hand, the effects of massive atomic strikes initiating the war were much *less* destructive than suggested above, either as a result of outlawing atomic weapons or as a result of effective defense measures, we would then have conditions of warfare more or less analogous to those of World War II, except for such differences as might result from the tactical use of atomic weapons and the employment of other new weapons systems developed since World War II. Under such conditions, the conventional methods of economic mobilization would be more or less applicable.

CONCLUSION

Prior to 1914 mobilization for war was almost wholly a military operation, involving little more than the raising, training, and equipping of troops and placing the trained units in the field ready for combat. Problems of providing the personnel, the equipment, and the supplies for these military forces presented many difficulties. Success in dealing with these problems had much to do with the outcome not only of battles and campaigns but of wars. Yet, with minor exceptions, positive measures by the Government to direct and manage the economic resources of the nation in support of military operations were unknown. Beyond the procurement of military equipment and supplies and the raising of funds through taxation and loans to pay for them, the Government did not interfere in the functioning of the economic system. The economy operated about the same during war as in peacetime, although, with military requirements added to ordinary civilian demands, there was usually a business boom accompanied by "prosperity" on the home front.

All this has changed during the past generation. So great is the scale, intensity, and mechanization of modern warfare that only the most advanced economies, operating at the highest attainable level of efficiency, can provide the materials and materiel for effective military operations. The full and rapid mobilization of military forces— ground, sea, and air—is in itself not enough. It must be accompanied and, if possible, preceded by the mobilization of the productive resources of the nation. Moreover, to mobilize these resources fully requires far more than placing unlimited financial resources at the disposal of the military for the procurement of their requirements. It demands nothing less than the planned and directed management of the national economy as a closely coordinated whole. In no other way can the production of the right kind of goods be maintained in the tremendous amounts necessary and on the time schedules essential for the execution of strategic plans.

Because of the close dependence of the military effort on civilian production, modern war is no longer waged, as it was to so large an extent for centuries, by the military alone.   It is waged by a military-civilian team which includes virtually the entire civilian population no less than the men and women in the Armed Forces.   It is waged, moreover, with machine tools and blast furnaces, with assembly lines and drafting instruments, with research laboratories and technical schools, with farms and factories, no less than with the military materiel which has increased so rapidly in number, in size and complexity, and in destructiveness.

Although it is the primary responsibility of the military to fight and of the civilians to produce, soldiers have important duties related to production and civilians are often found in the front line of aerial offensives.   In the procurement and utilization of their vast requirements of munitions and other supplies, the armed services must avoid wastes that will weaken and demands that will impair the strength, that is, productiveness, of the civilian economy on which the war effort is based.   In their turn, civilians must accept not only the material sacrifices but the restrictions on the freedom of their economic behavior that are essential both to reduce civilian consumption and to increase production to the highest feasible levels and to maintain the stability of the economic system which is so essential to the attainment of maximum production.

Clearly, the American people have come a long way during the past generation, both in their experience with war and in their attitudes toward the preparation and planning for the possibility of war. Through bitter experience, they have come to realize that a democracy must be prepared at all times with plans for dealing with the eventuality of war, whether hot or cold, limited, or total, and that these plans must cover the economic no less than the military aspects of mobilization. Statutory organizations, civilian no less than military, have been evolved to carry on planning activities and much care, thought, and money have been devoted to the conduct of this work. To the experience of the 1930's in planning for economic mobilization has been added the very different planning experience of the years between the end of World War II and the outbreak of the Korean war.   A test of this planning, resulting in modifications of some of its concepts, was afforded through its implementation to cope with the partial mobilization of the Korean war itself.   From all this experi-. ence a few things of importance, at least, have been learned: That the conditions and problems of economic mobilization are in process of continuous change; that planning is a task which is never finished; that there are no ready answers and no final solutions; and that the scale and the complexity of the problems in this field may be expected steadily to increase.   Eternal vigilance is the price, not only of individual liberty, but of national security.

BIBLIOGRAPHY

Baruch, Bernard M., *American Industry in the War. A Report of the War Industries Board*, New York: Prentice-Hall, 1941.

Civilian Production Administration, *Industrial Mobilization. History of the War Production Board and Predecessor Agencies 1940-1945*, Vol. I, Program and Administration. Washington, D. C.: Government Printing Office, 1947.

Clark, John Maurice, *The Costs of the World War to the American People*, New Haven: Yale University Press, 1931.

Clarkson, Grosvenor B., *Industrial America in the World War*, Boston: Houghton, Mifflin & Co., 1924.

Mock, James R., and Thurber, E. W., *Report on Demobilization*, Oklahoma City: University of Oklahoma Press, 1944.

Ramsdell, Charles W., *Behind the Lines in the Confederacy*, Baton Rouge, La.: Louisiana State University Press, 1944.

United Nations, *Statistical Yearbook*, New York, United Nations. (Yearly publication.)

U. S. Bureau of the Budget, *The United States at War, Development and Administration of the War Program of the Federal Government*, Washington, D. C.: Government Printing Office, 1946.

U. S. Congress, *Trends in Economic Growth*, 83d Cong., 2nd Sess., Joint Committee Print, 1955.

Wright, Chester W., *Economic History of the United States*, New York: McGraw-Hill Book Co., 1949.

Yoshpe, Harry B., *Plans for Industrial Mobilization 1920-1939*, Washington, D. C.: ICAF, 1945.

INDEX

www.ingramcontent.com/pod-product-compliance
Lightning Source LLC
Chambersburg PA
CBHW022124280326
41933CB00007B/534